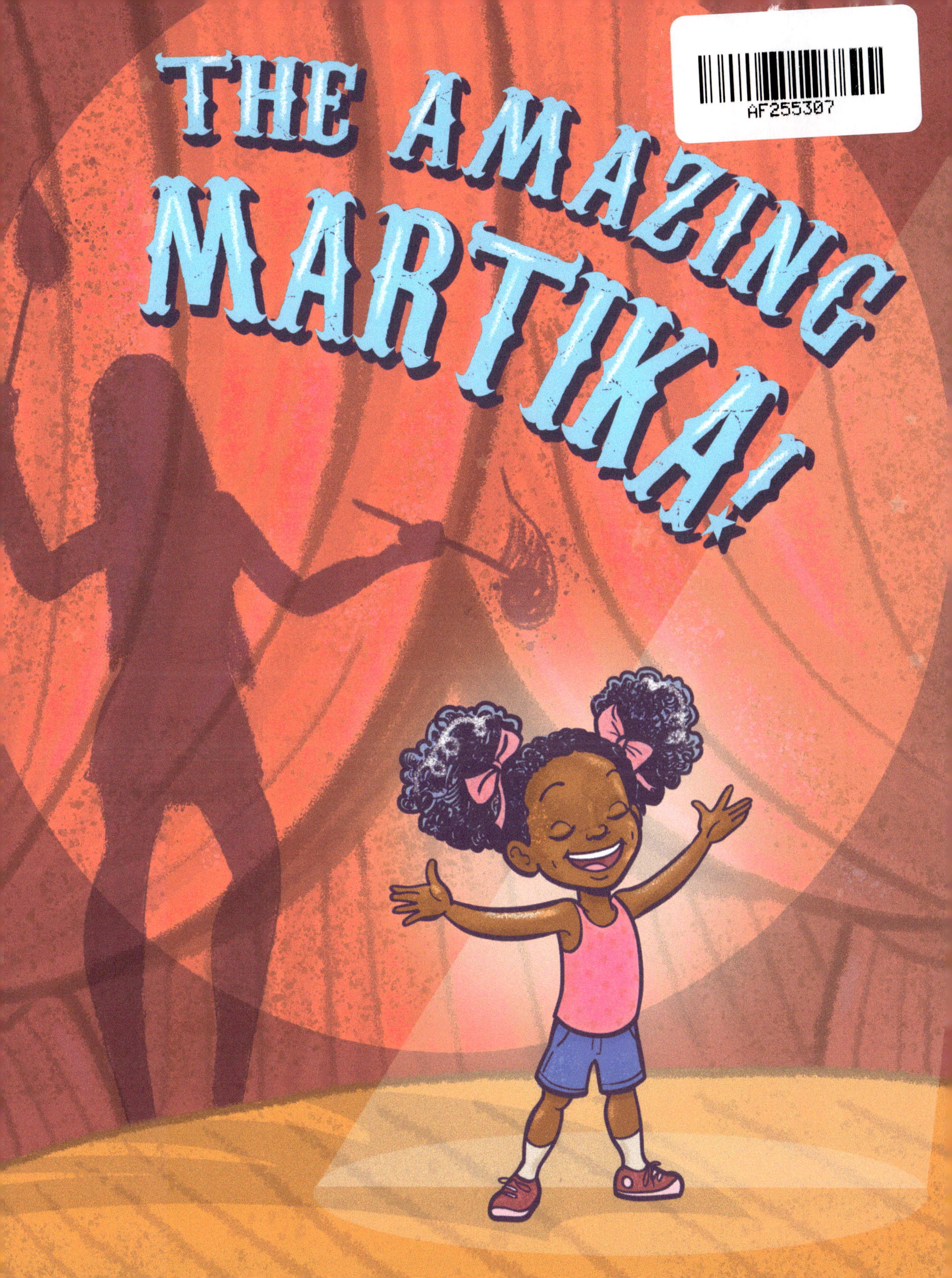

THE AMAZING MARTIKA!
AF255307

I dedicate this book to my family
and friends that have supported
me along the way.

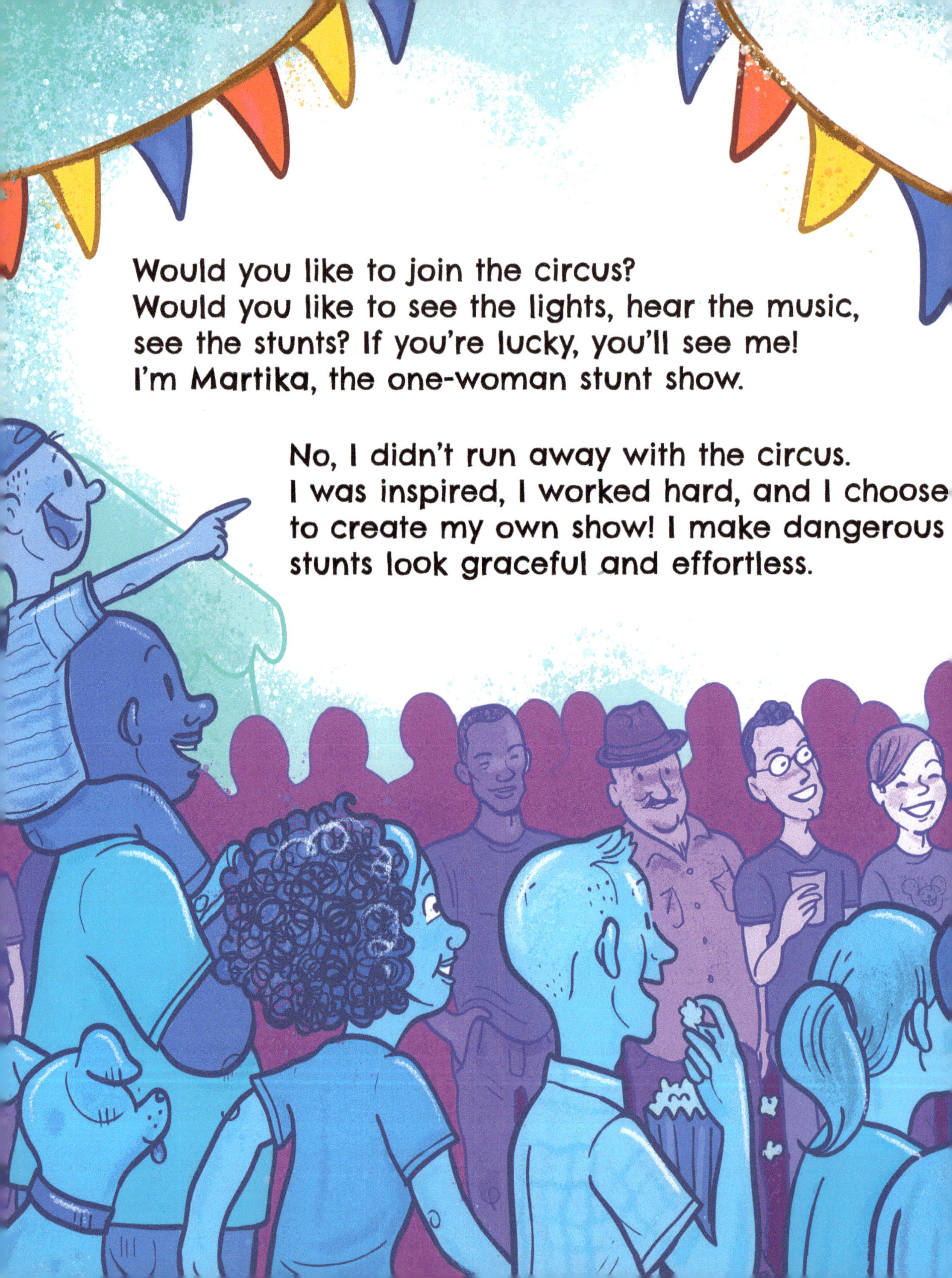

Would you like to join the circus?
Would you like to see the lights, hear the music,
see the stunts? If you're lucky, you'll see me!
I'm Martika, the one-woman stunt show.

No, I didn't run away with the circus.
I was inspired, I worked hard, and I choose
to create my own show! I make dangerous
stunts look graceful and effortless.

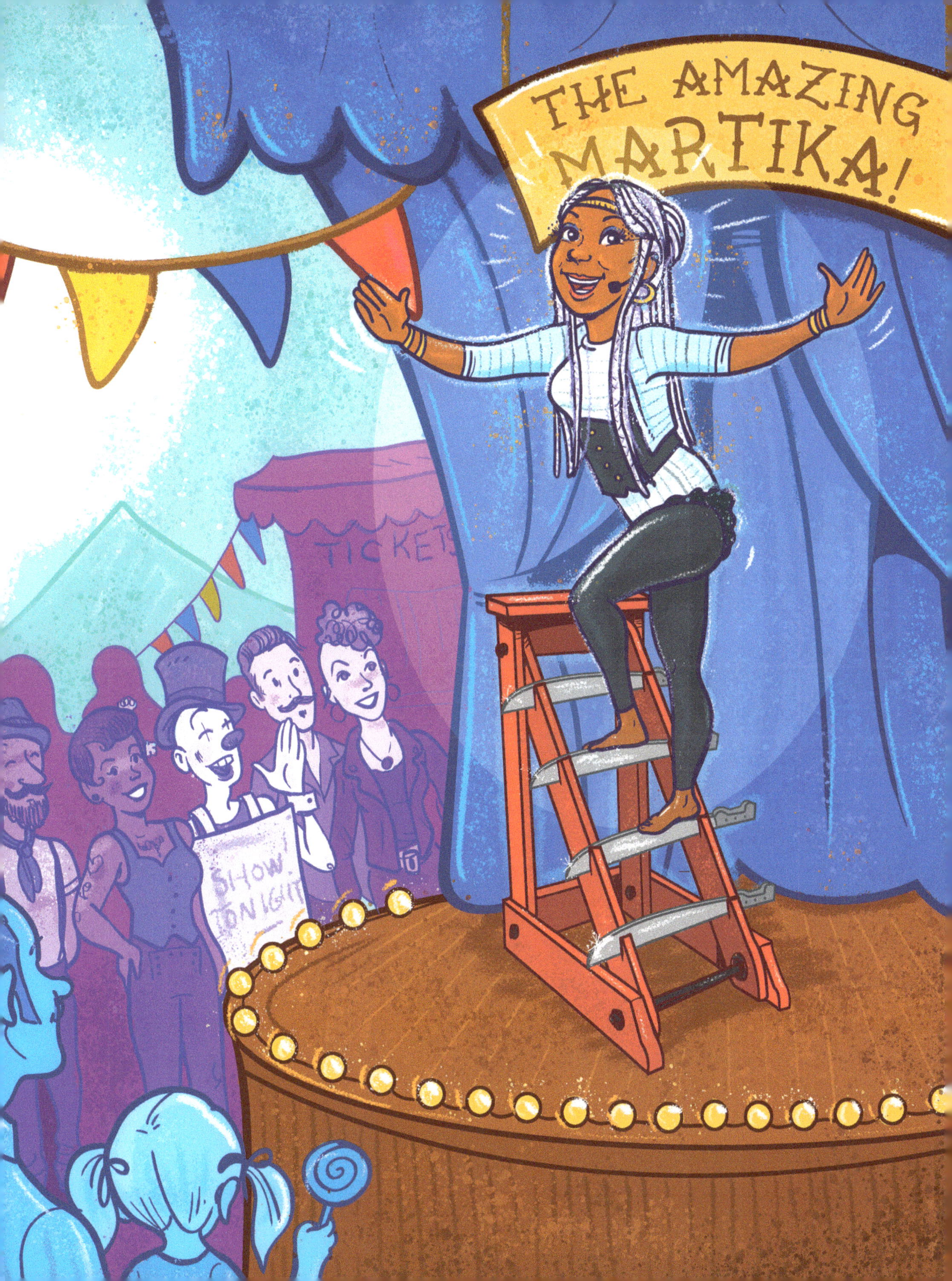

THE AMAZING MARTIKA!
SHOW TONIGHT
TICKETS

I have had anything but a normal upbringing! I grew up with a father in the United States Air Force, and his job took us all over the world.

From Florida to Nebraska, then to Germany and California, and finally to Kansas.

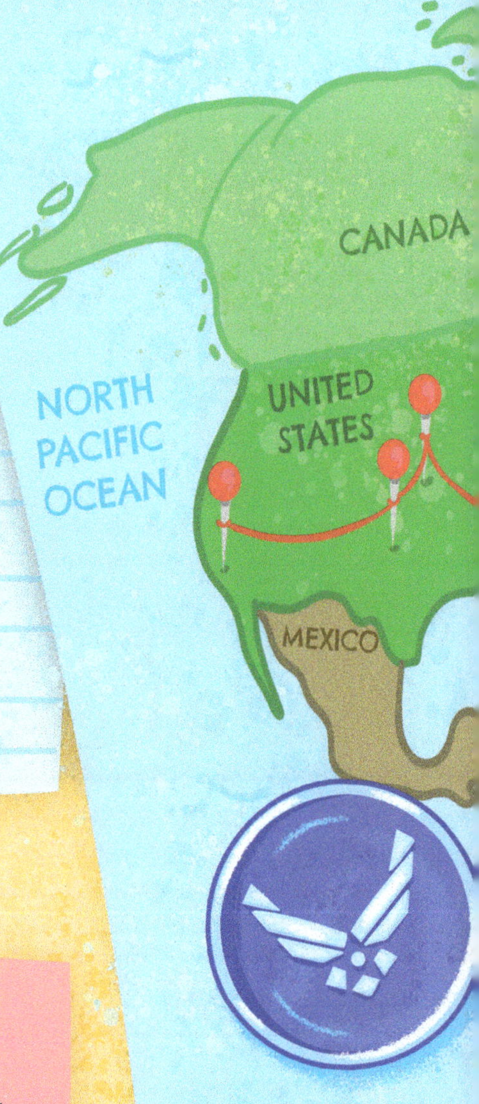

Even though my parents worked very hard for my family, they still made time for my siblings and I. We were very lucky to spend our family vacations in places like France, Italy, Switzerland, Luxembourg, and Germany.

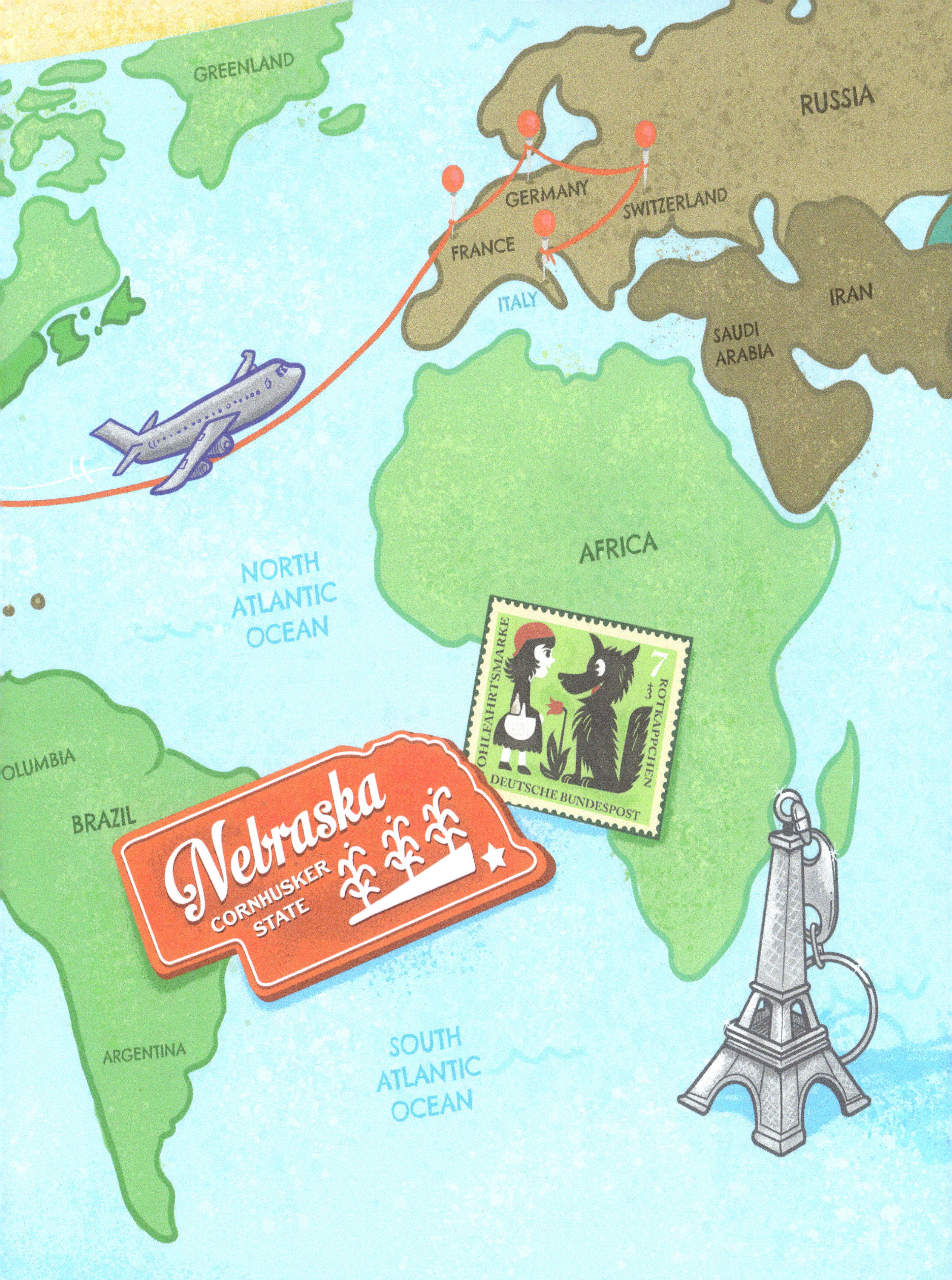

GREENLAND
RUSSIA
GERMANY
FRANCE
SWITZERLAND
ITALY
IRAN
SAUDI ARABIA
AFRICA
NORTH ATLANTIC OCEAN
COLUMBIA
BRAZIL
ARGENTINA
SOUTH ATLANTIC OCEAN
Nebraska
CORNHUSKER STATE
WOHLFAHRTSMARKE
ROTKÄPPCHEN
7
DEUTSCHE BUNDESPOST

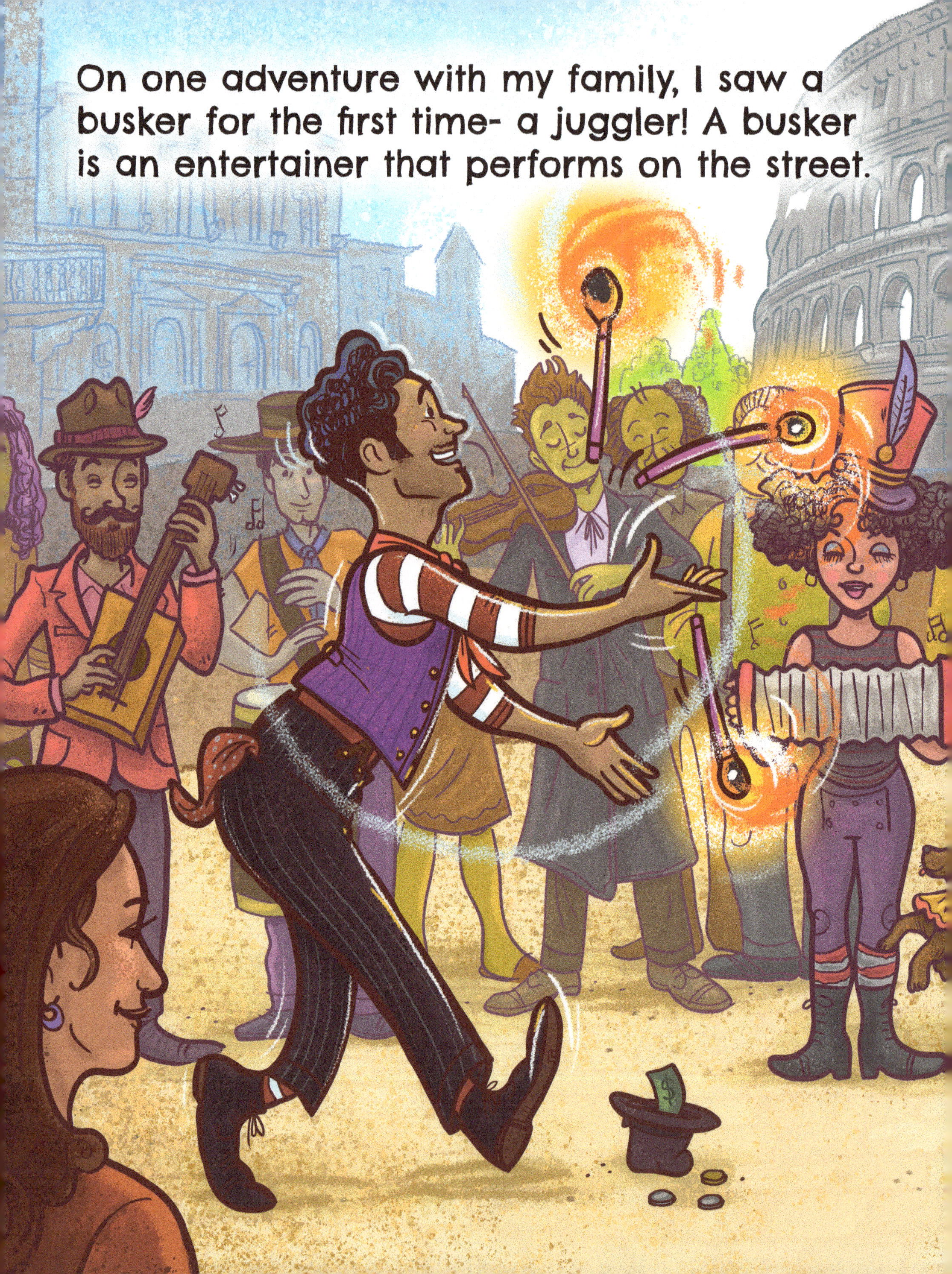

On one adventure with my family, I saw a busker for the first time- a juggler! A busker is an entertainer that performs on the street.

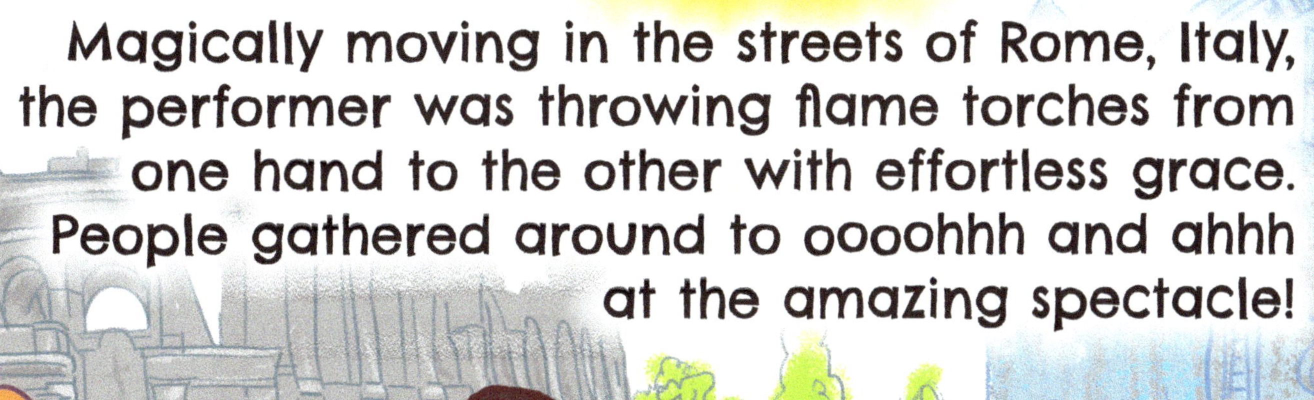
Magically moving in the streets of Rome, Italy, the performer was throwing flame torches from one hand to the other with effortless grace. People gathered around to oooohhh and ahhh at the amazing spectacle!

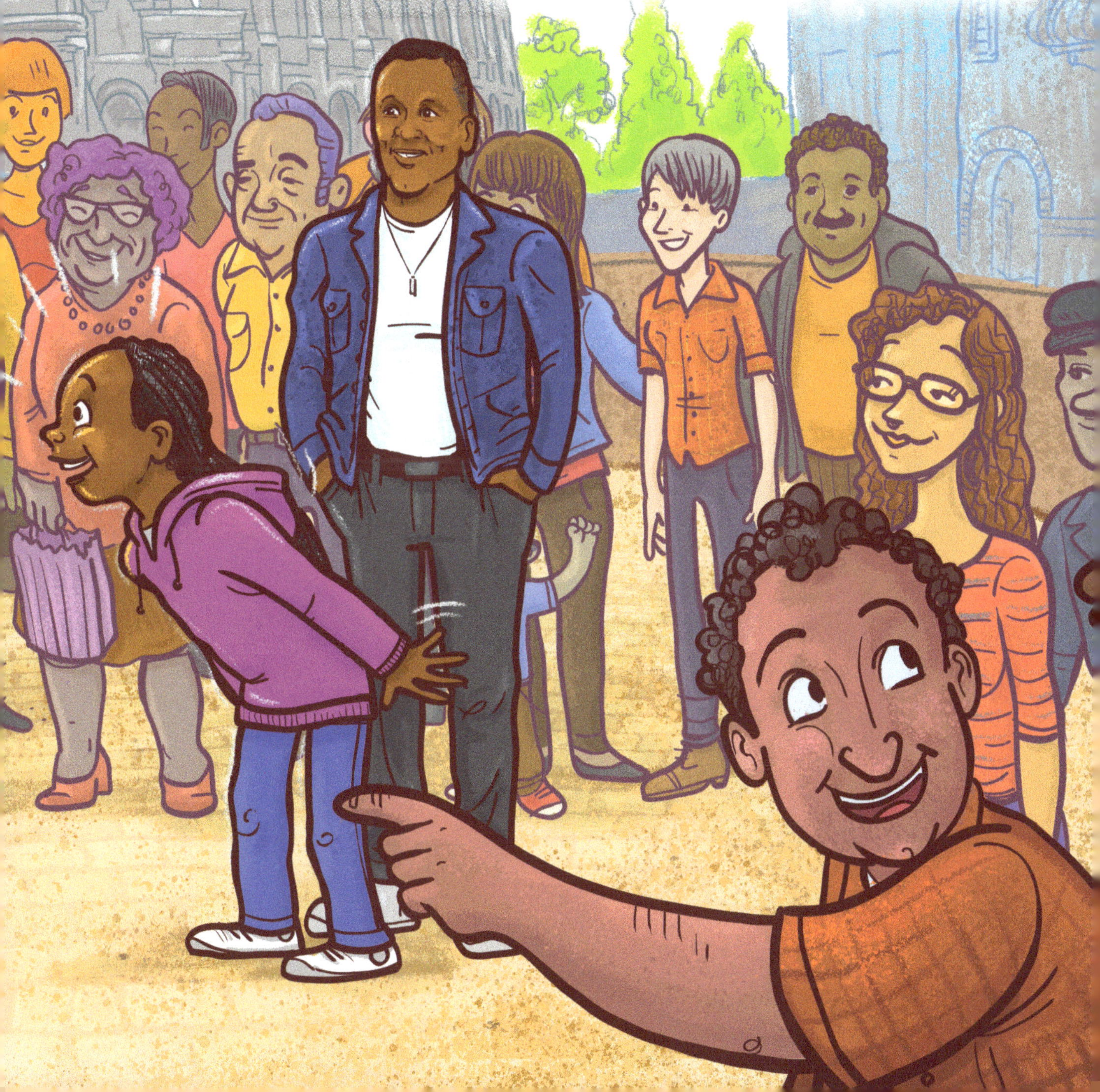

I discovered that there are other kinds of performance arts. Acts like fire eating, escapology, and sideshow stunts, like sword swallowing. The more I read, the more history I found. I learned about performers that look like me. Black performers showcasing their amazing talents and doing incredible feats of danger.

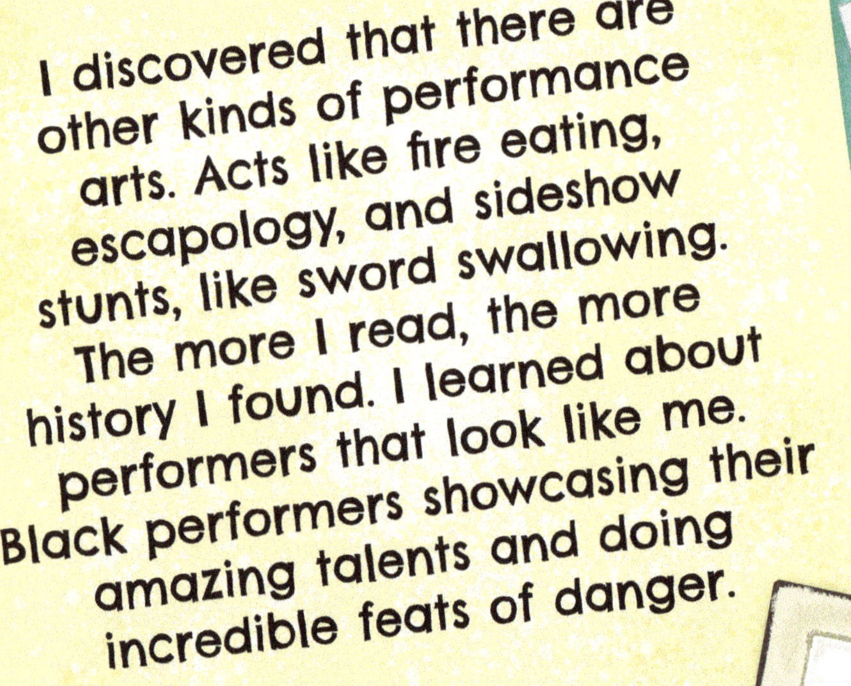

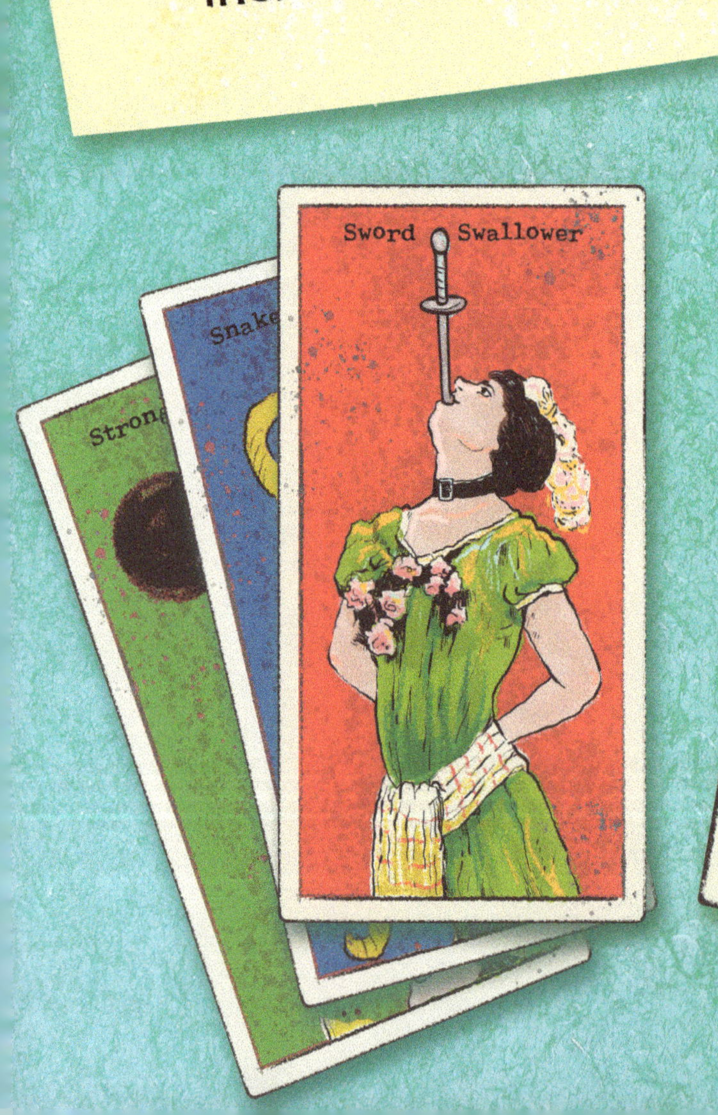

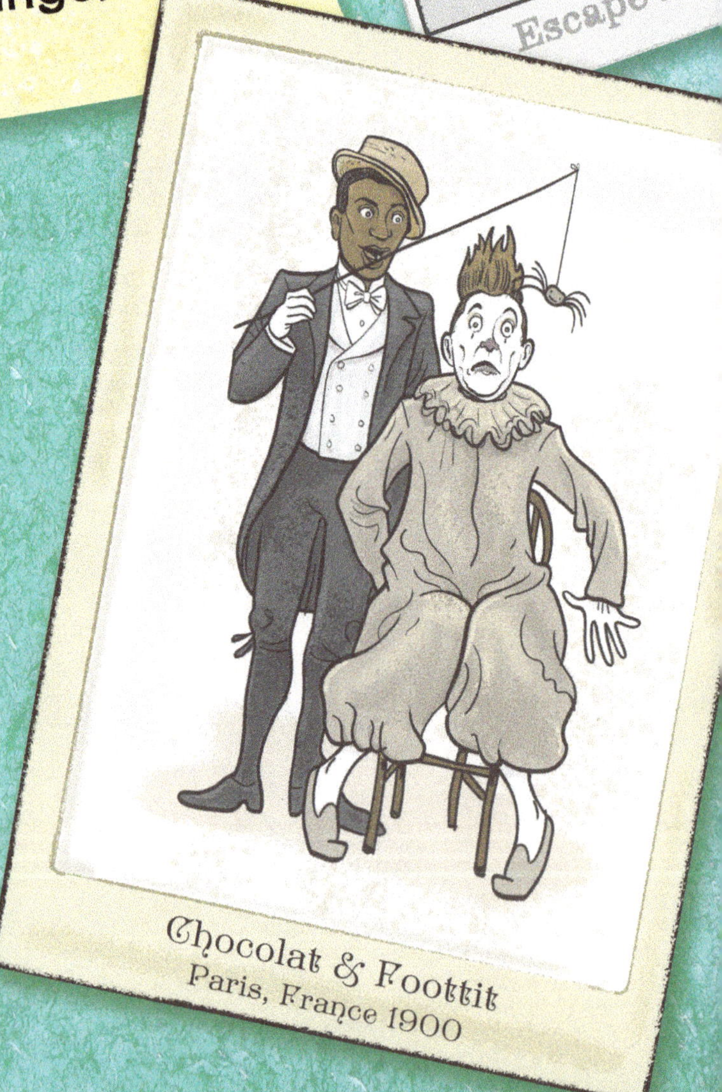

Circus and sideshow history have a glamorous side and a dark side. The Muse Brothers were taken from their home against their will and sold to a circus ringmaster. When I learned these brothers' story, I admired their strength.

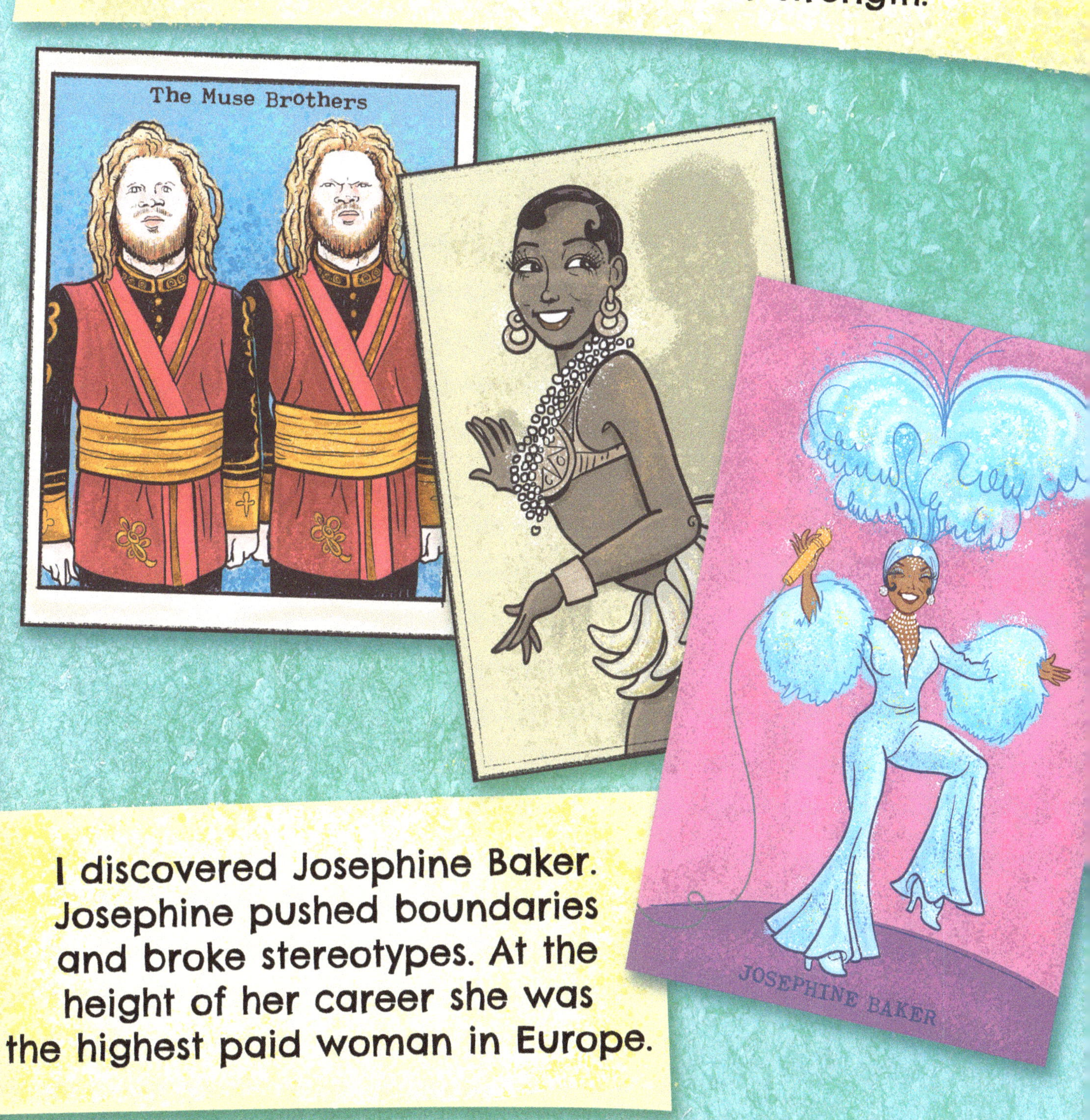

I discovered Josephine Baker. Josephine pushed boundaries and broke stereotypes. At the height of her career she was the highest paid woman in Europe.

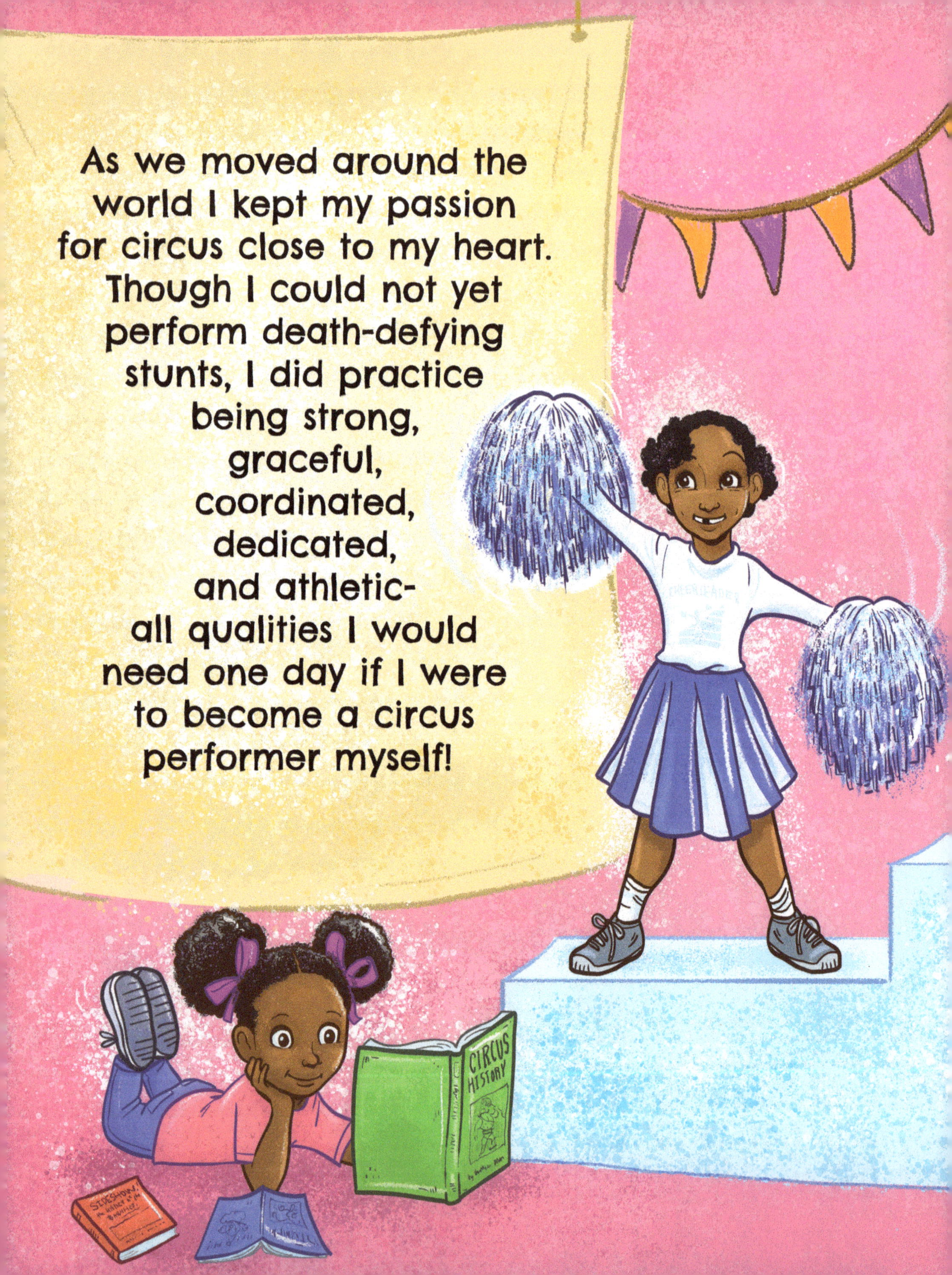As we moved around the world I kept my passion for circus close to my heart. Though I could not yet perform death-defying stunts, I did practice being strong, graceful, coordinated, dedicated, and athletic—all qualities I would need one day if I were to become a circus performer myself!

CIRCUS HISTORY

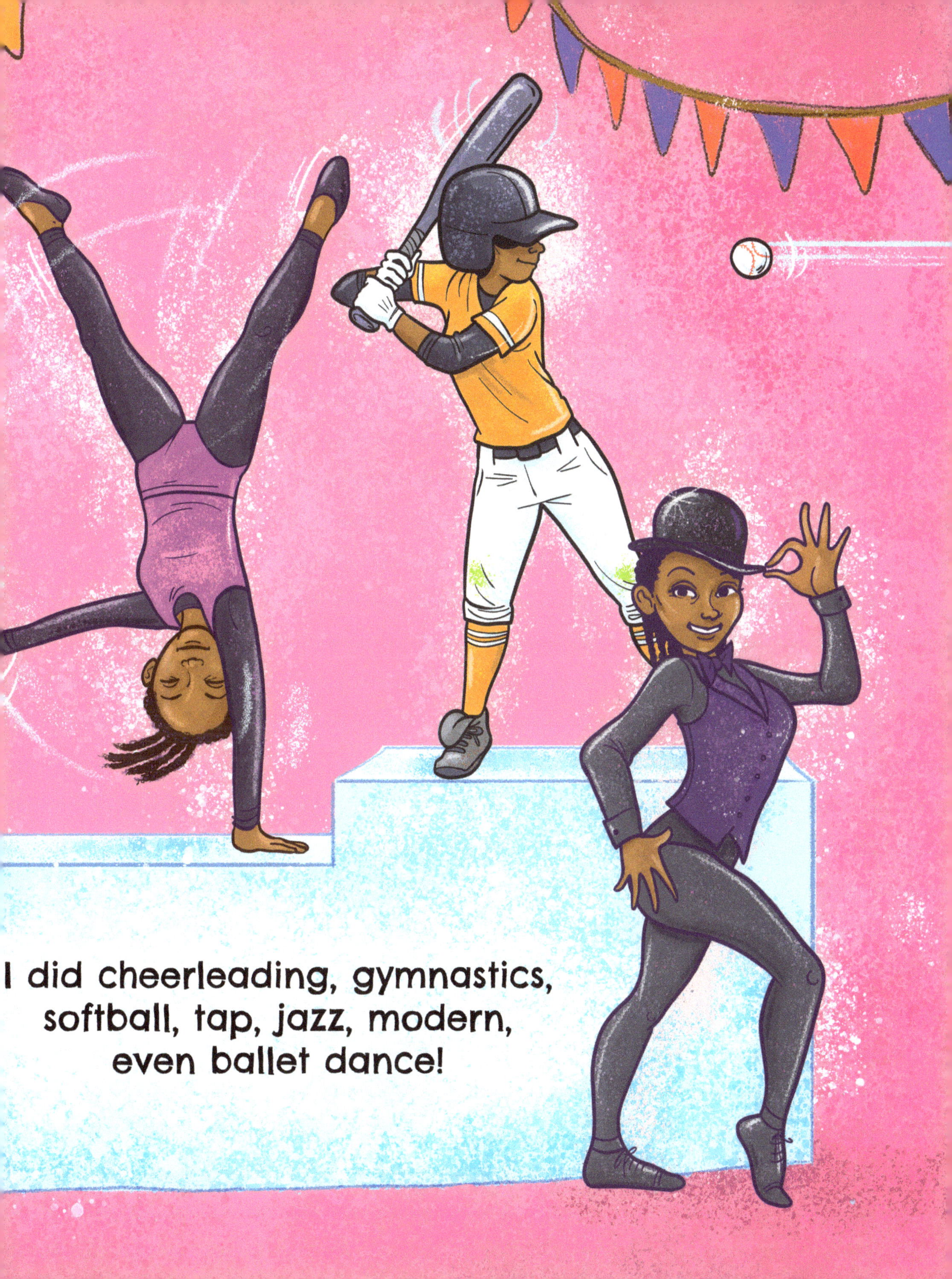

I did cheerleading, gymnastics, softball, tap, jazz, modern, even ballet dance!

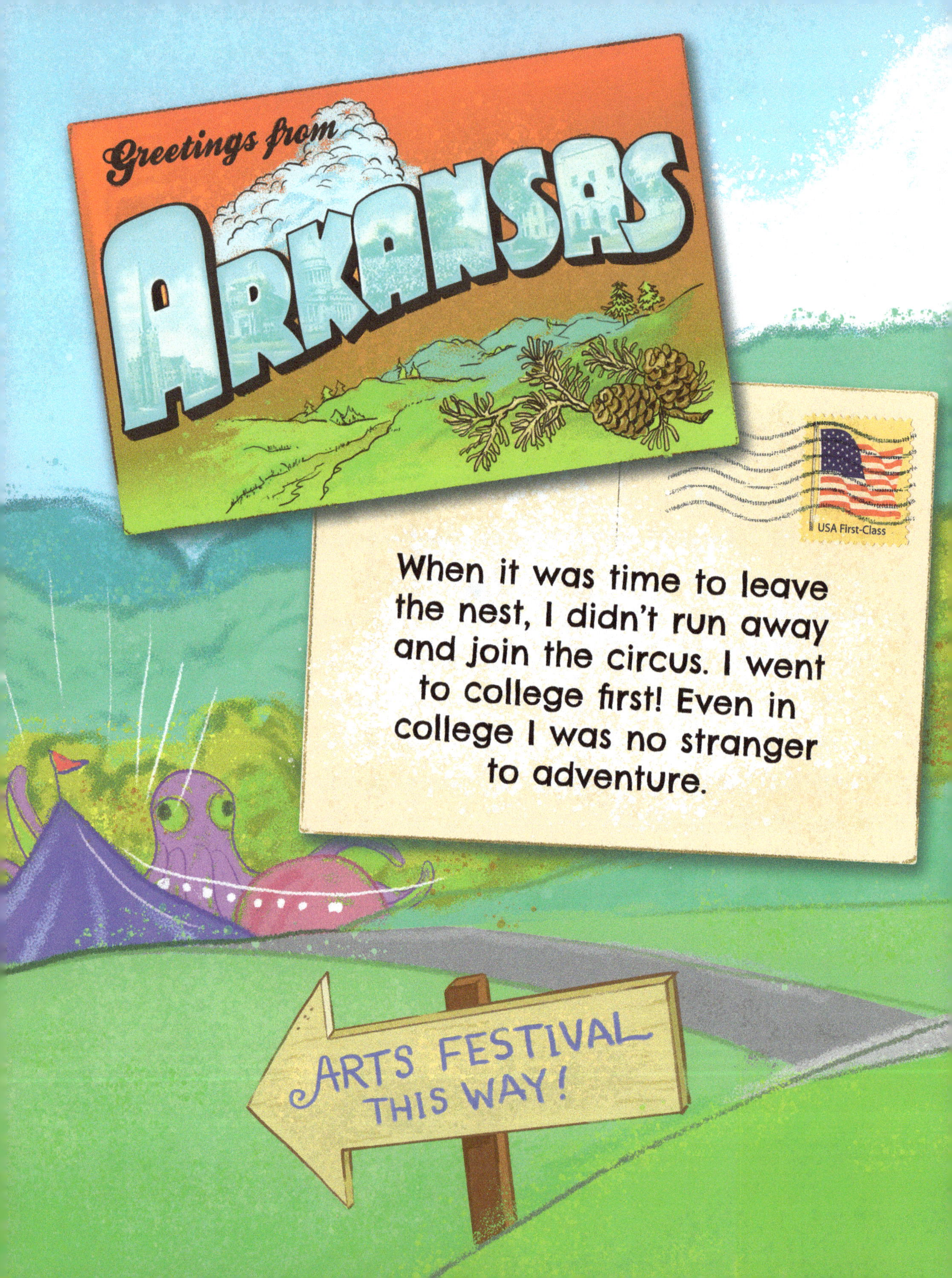

Greetings from
ARKANSAS
USA First-Class
When it was time to leave the nest, I didn't run away and join the circus. I went to college first! Even in college I was no stranger to adventure.
ARTS FESTIVAL THIS WAY!

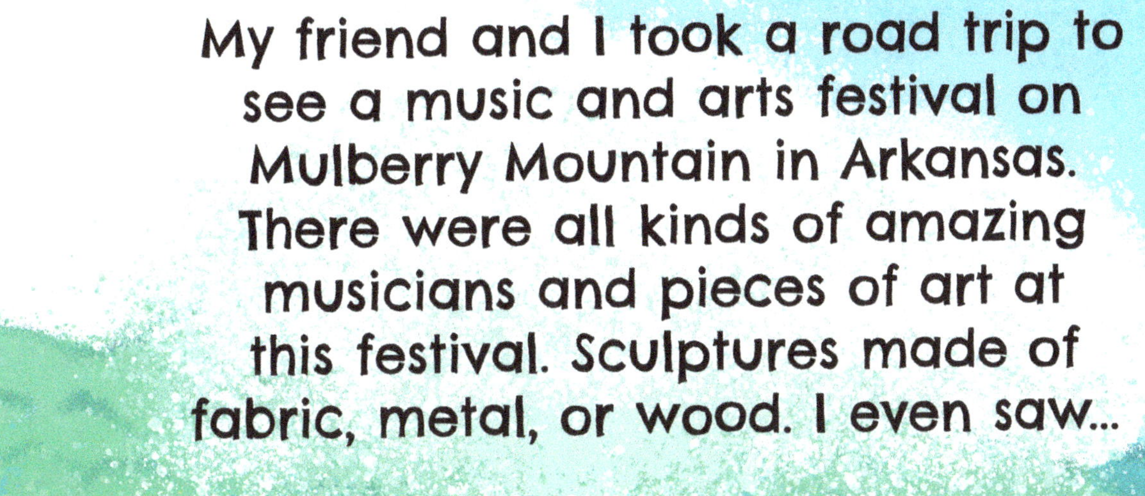

My friend and I took a road trip to see a music and arts festival on Mulberry Mountain in Arkansas. There were all kinds of amazing musicians and pieces of art at this festival. Sculptures made of fabric, metal, or wood. I even saw...

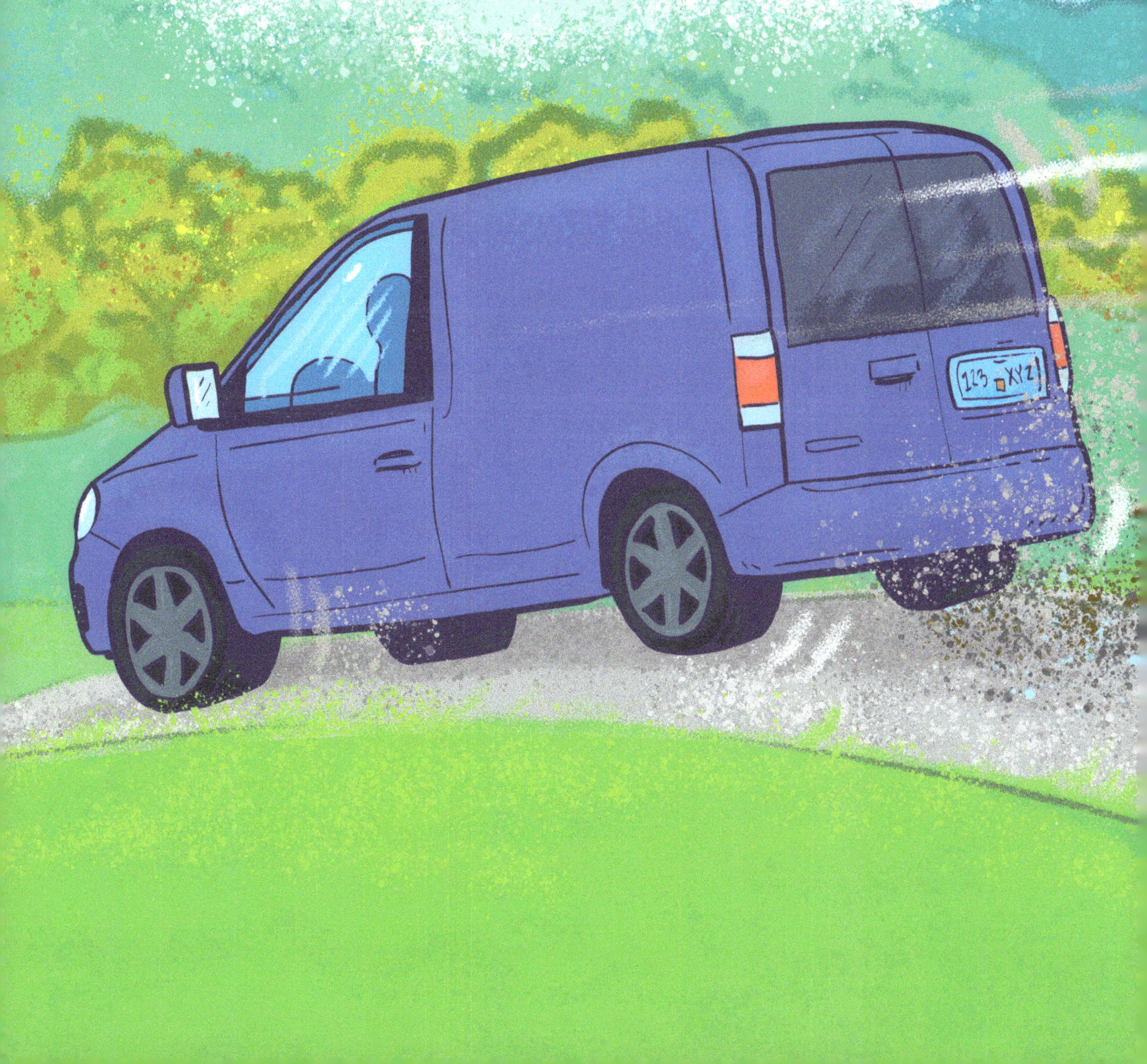

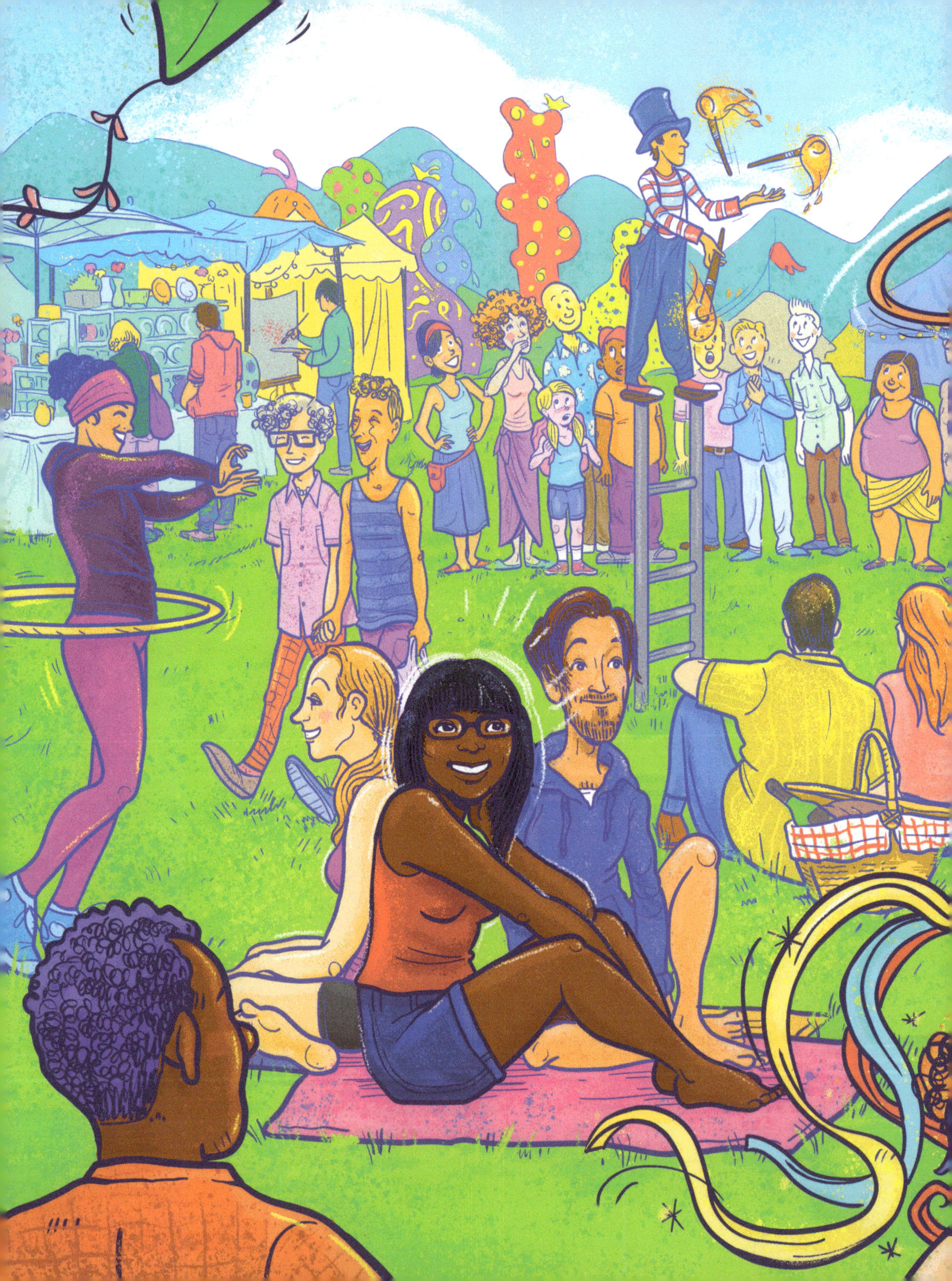

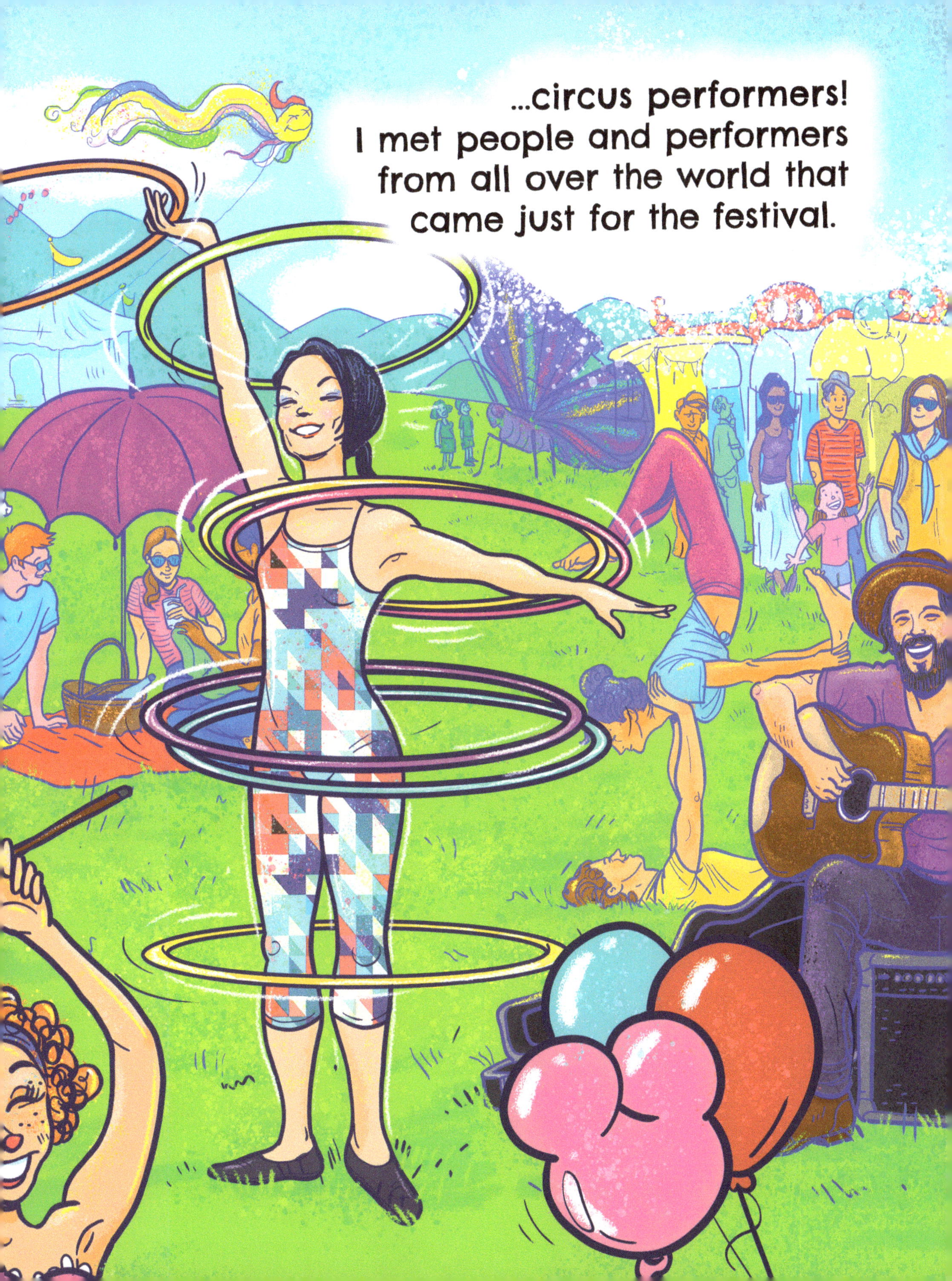
...circus performers!
I met people and performers
from all over the world that
came just for the festival.

Seeing these people live their dreams sparked a fire
in my belly. I was ready to live my passion too! It had
been ten years since the first time I saw a circus
performer in real life. This time, I wanted to take
advantage and ask the performer some questions.
As soon as the performer was finished
I rushed over with wonder and awe.

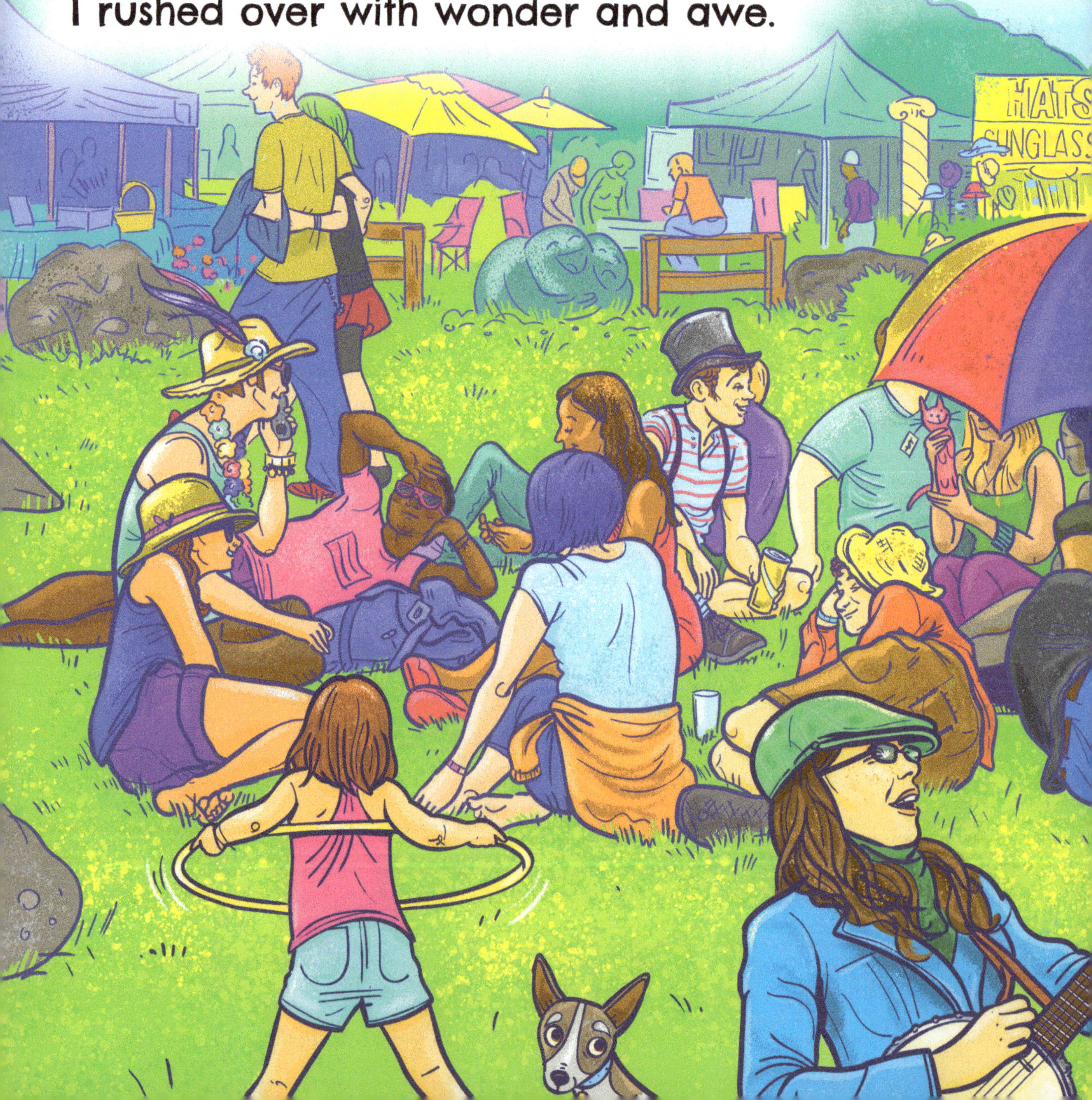

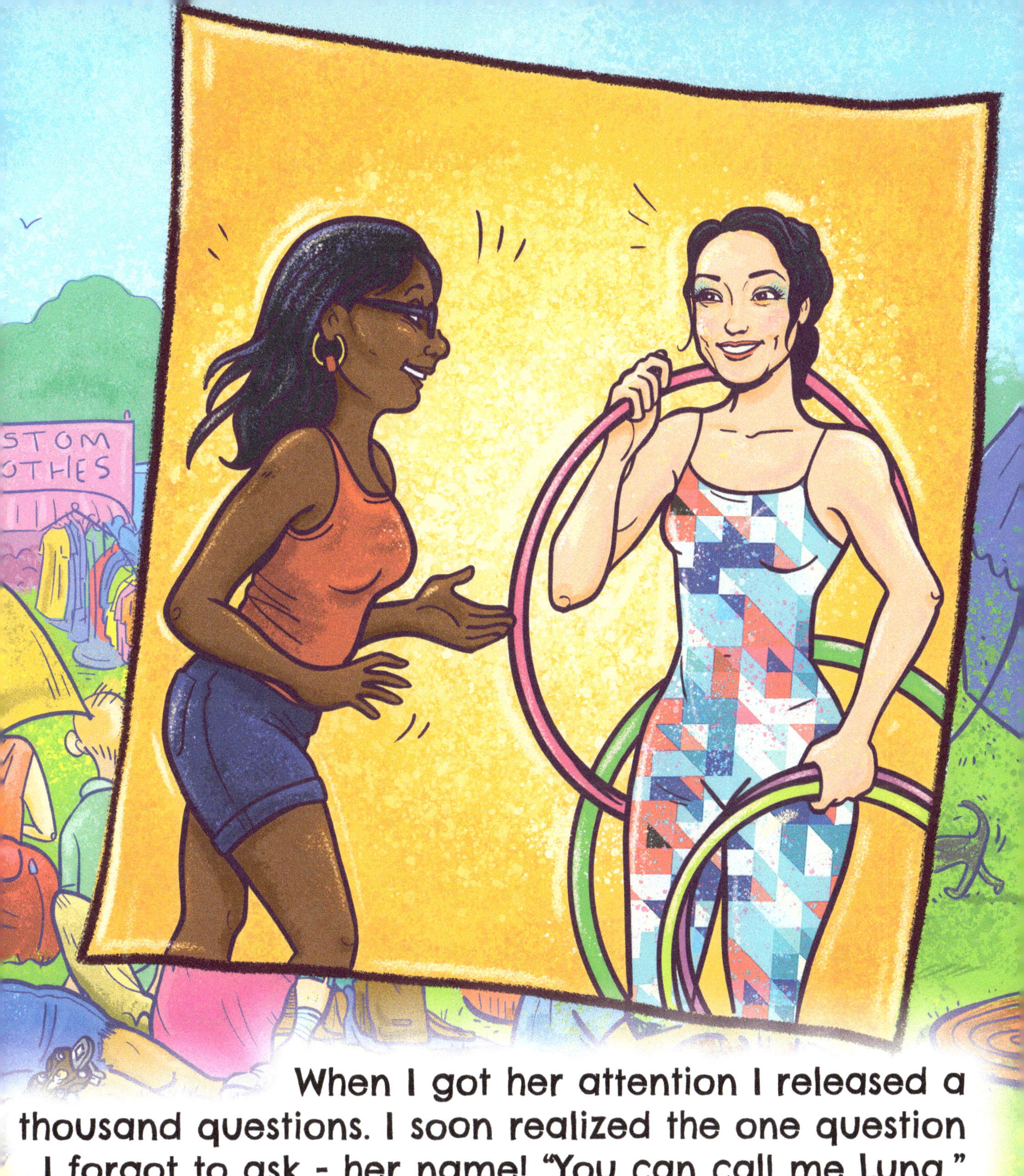

When I got her attention I released a thousand questions. I soon realized the one question I forgot to ask - her name! "You can call me Luna," she said with a smile. "I am teaching hula hoop classes tomorrow. You should come. You will need a hula hoop."

I rushed around the festival all day looking for the perfect hula hoop. Many fine venders had hats, ribbons, stickers, rainbow hula hoops, and more.

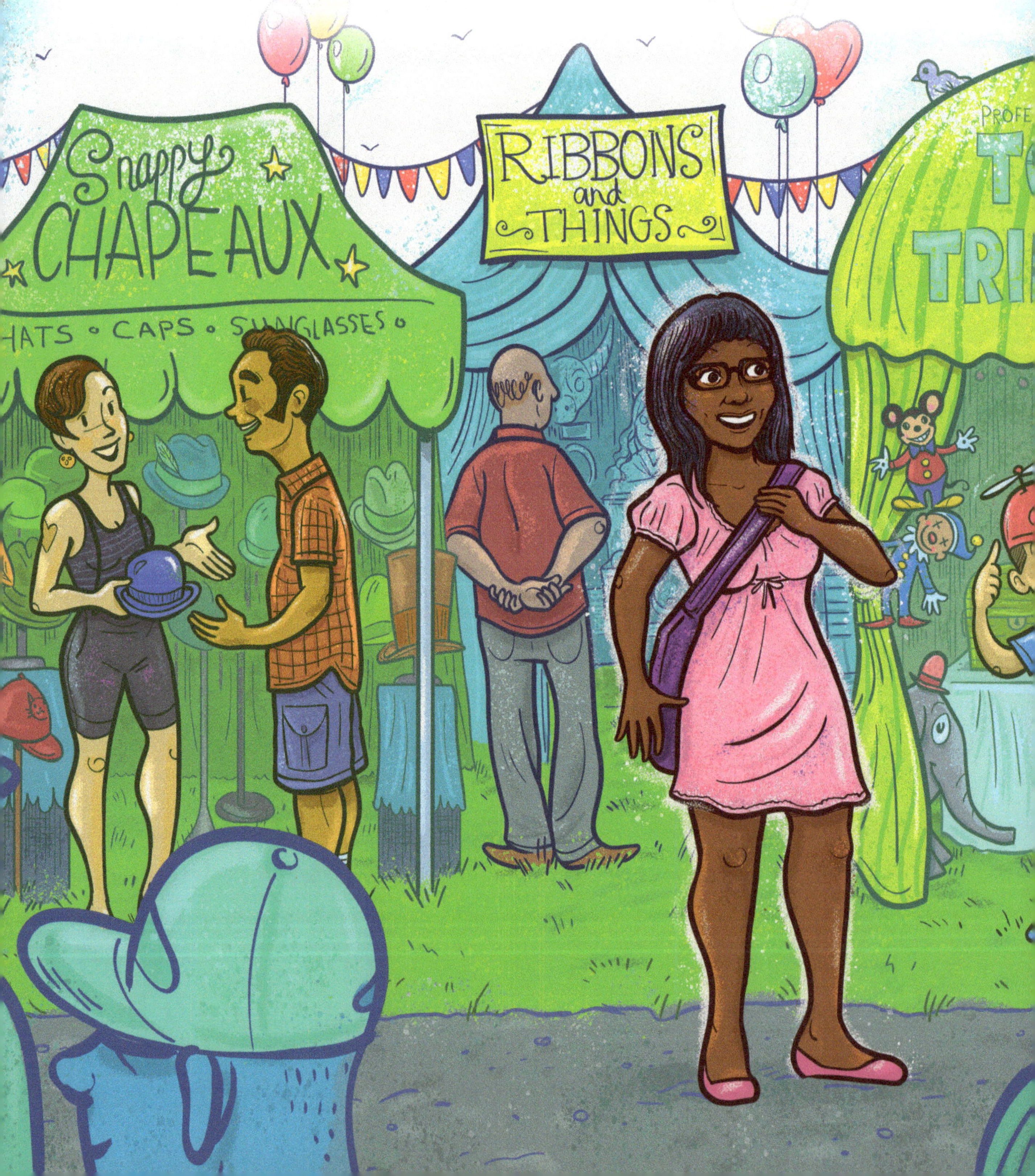

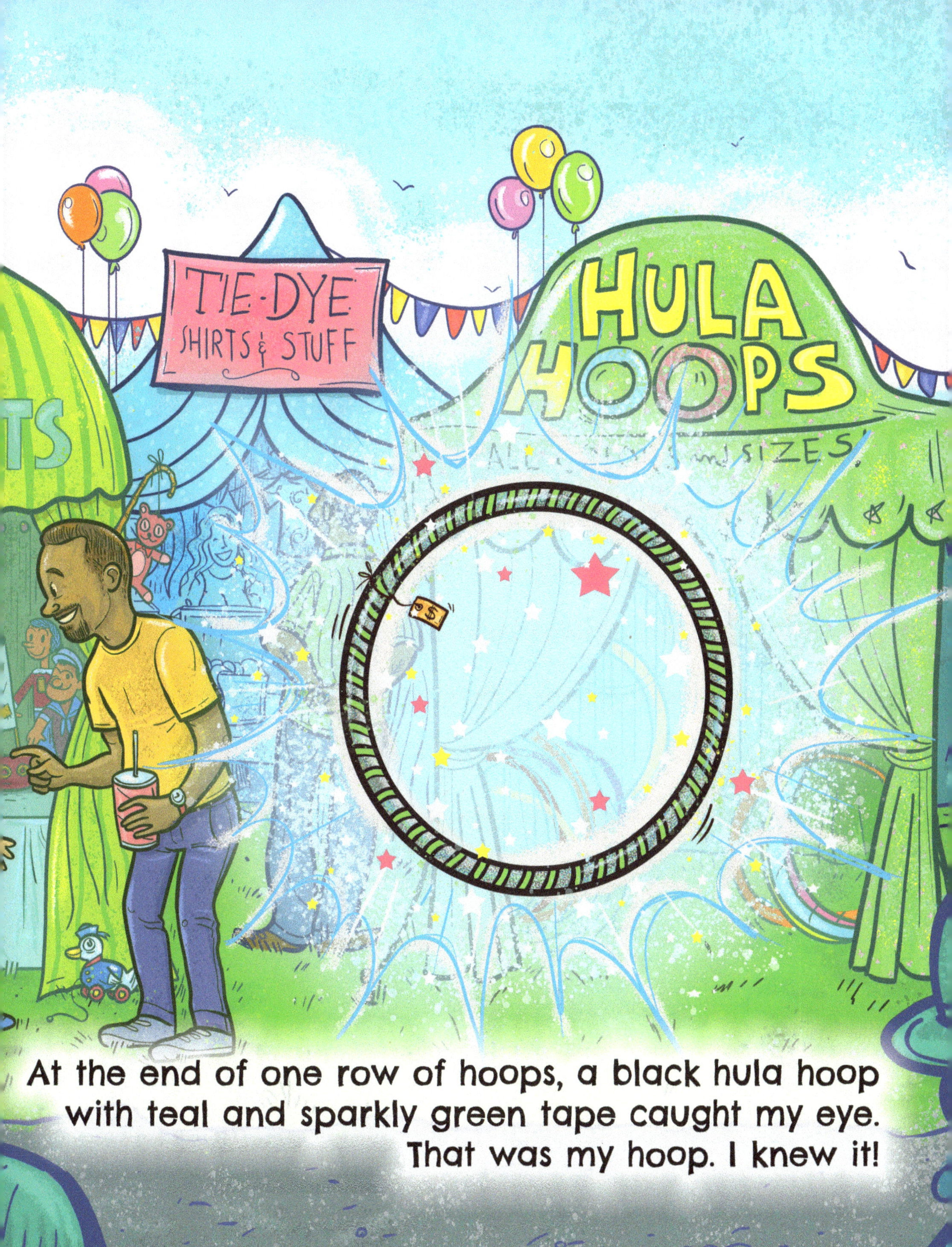

At the end of one row of hoops, a black hula hoop with teal and sparkly green tape caught my eye. That was my hoop. I knew it!

The hula hoop class was a struggle, big time!
I dropped the hoop over and over. I even hit
myself in the face with the hoop!
But I did not give up.

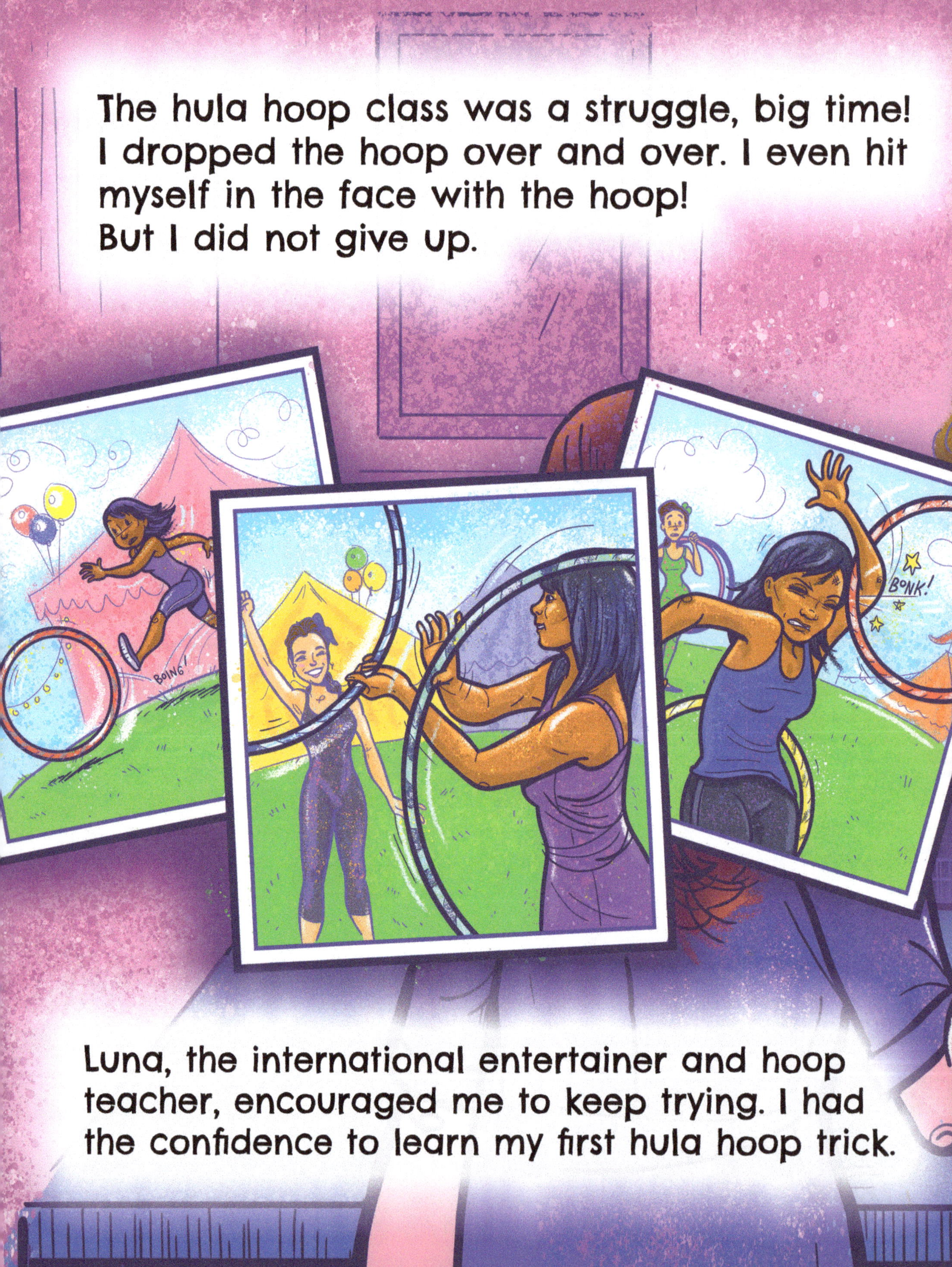

Luna, the international entertainer and hoop
teacher, encouraged me to keep trying. I had
the confidence to learn my first hula hoop trick.

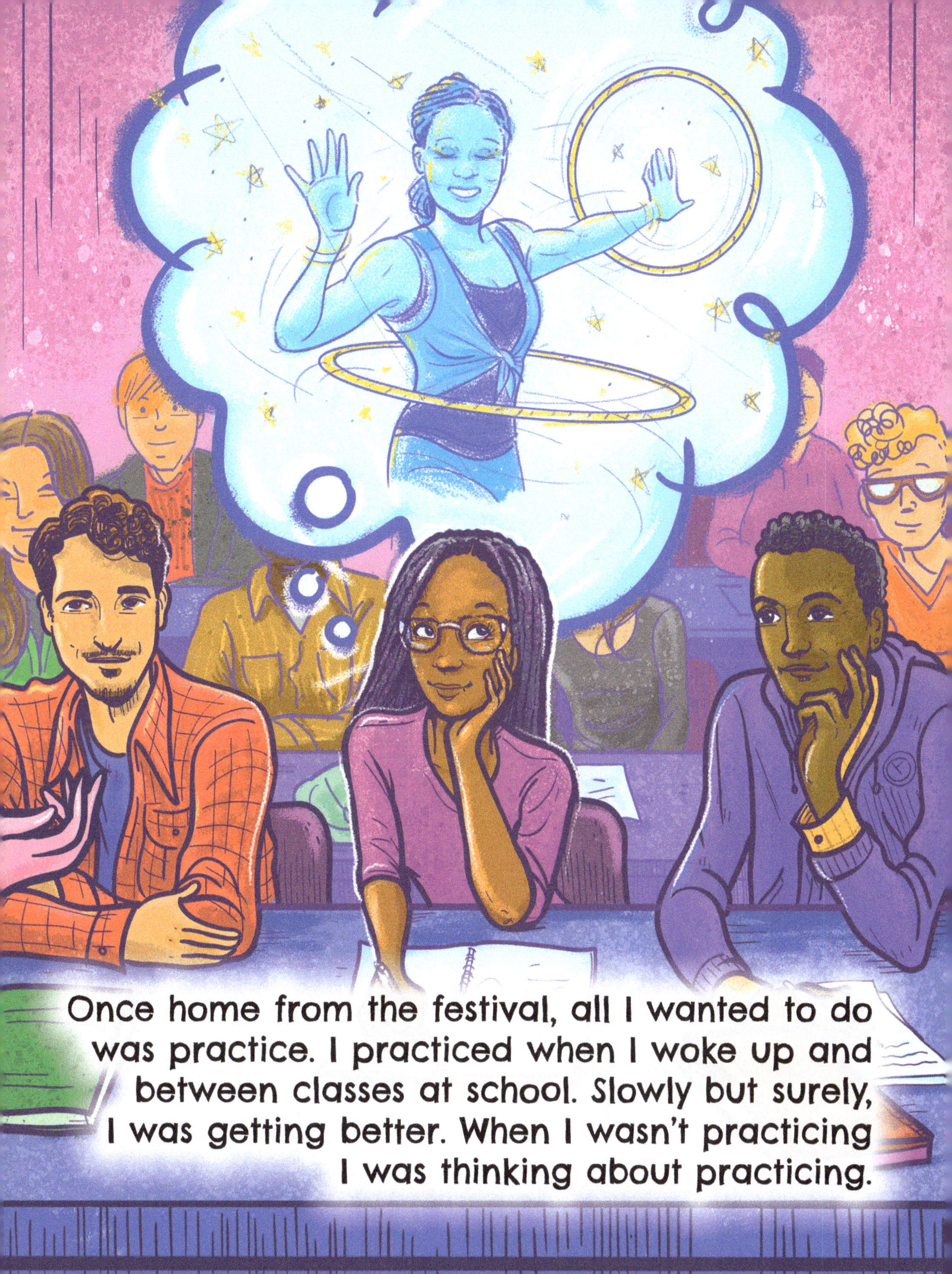Once home from the festival, all I wanted to do was practice. I practiced when I woke up and between classes at school. Slowly but surely, I was getting better. When I wasn't practicing I was thinking about practicing.

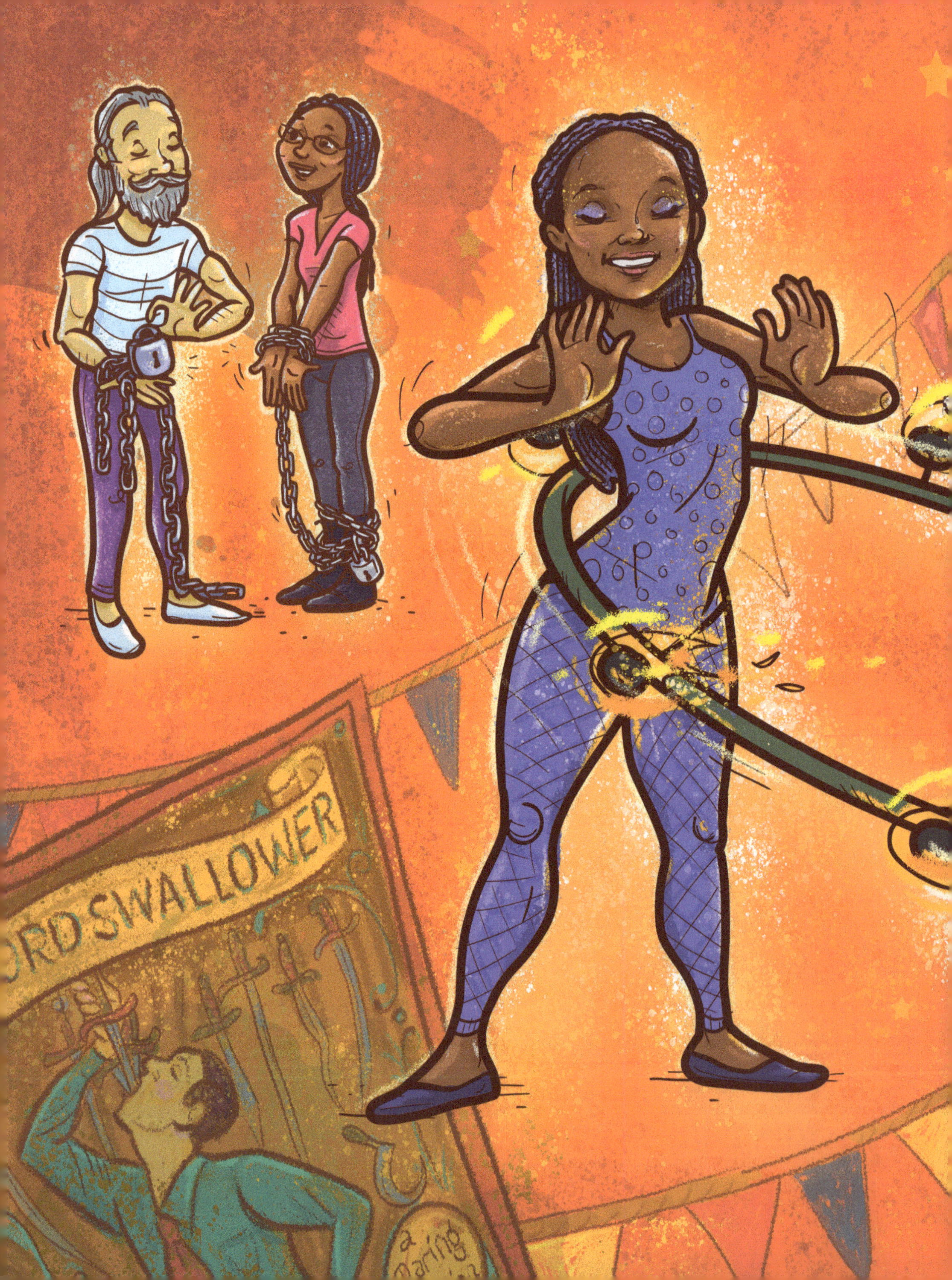
ORD SWALLOWER

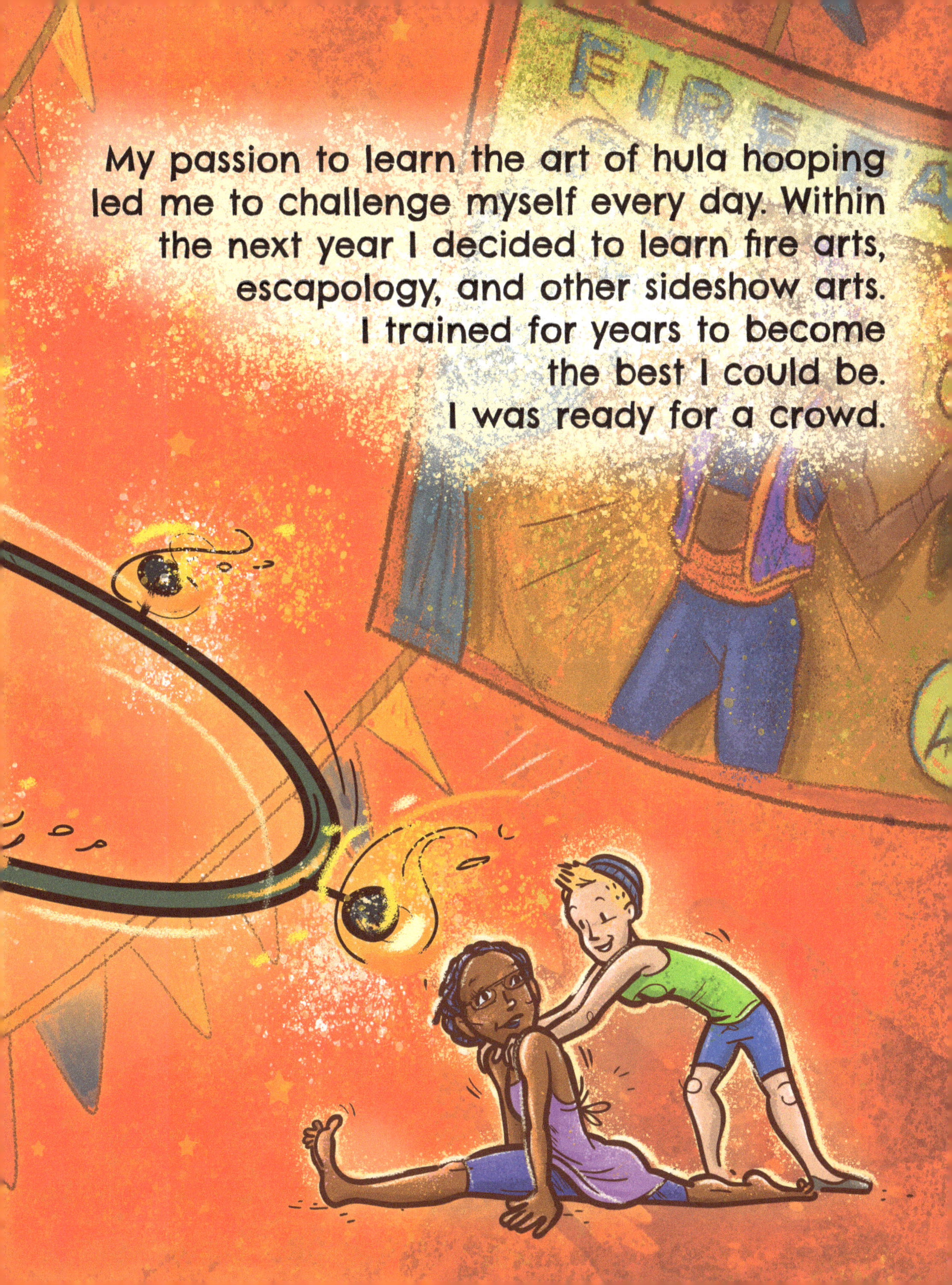

My passion to learn the art of hula hooping
led me to challenge myself every day. Within
the next year I decided to learn fire arts,
escapology, and other sideshow arts.
I trained for years to become
the best I could be.
I was ready for a crowd.

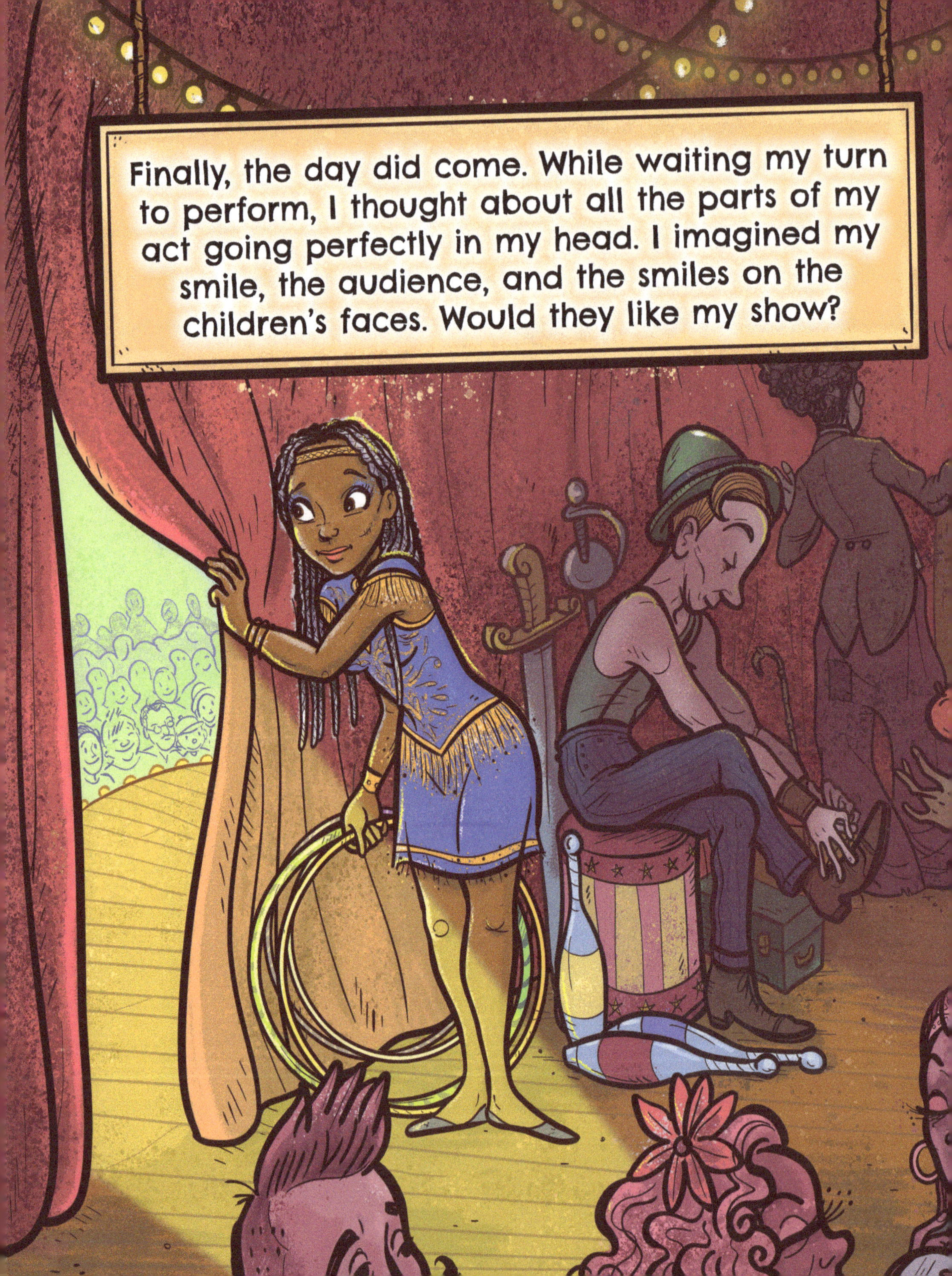
Finally, the day did come. While waiting my turn to perform, I thought about all the parts of my act going perfectly in my head. I imagined my smile, the audience, and the smiles on the children's faces. Would they like my show?

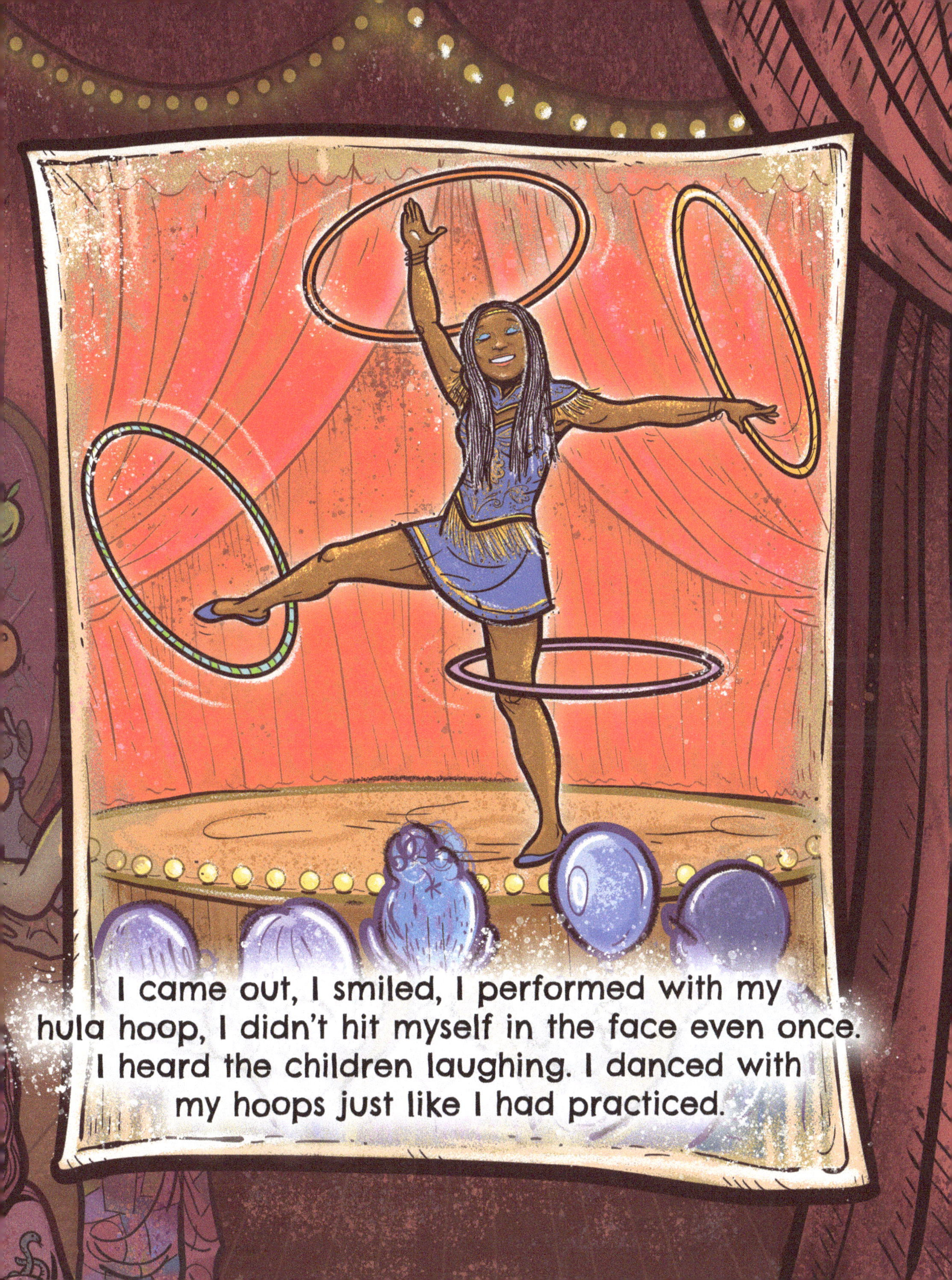

I came out, I smiled, I performed with my hula hoop, I didn't hit myself in the face even once. I heard the children laughing. I danced with my hoops just like I had practiced.

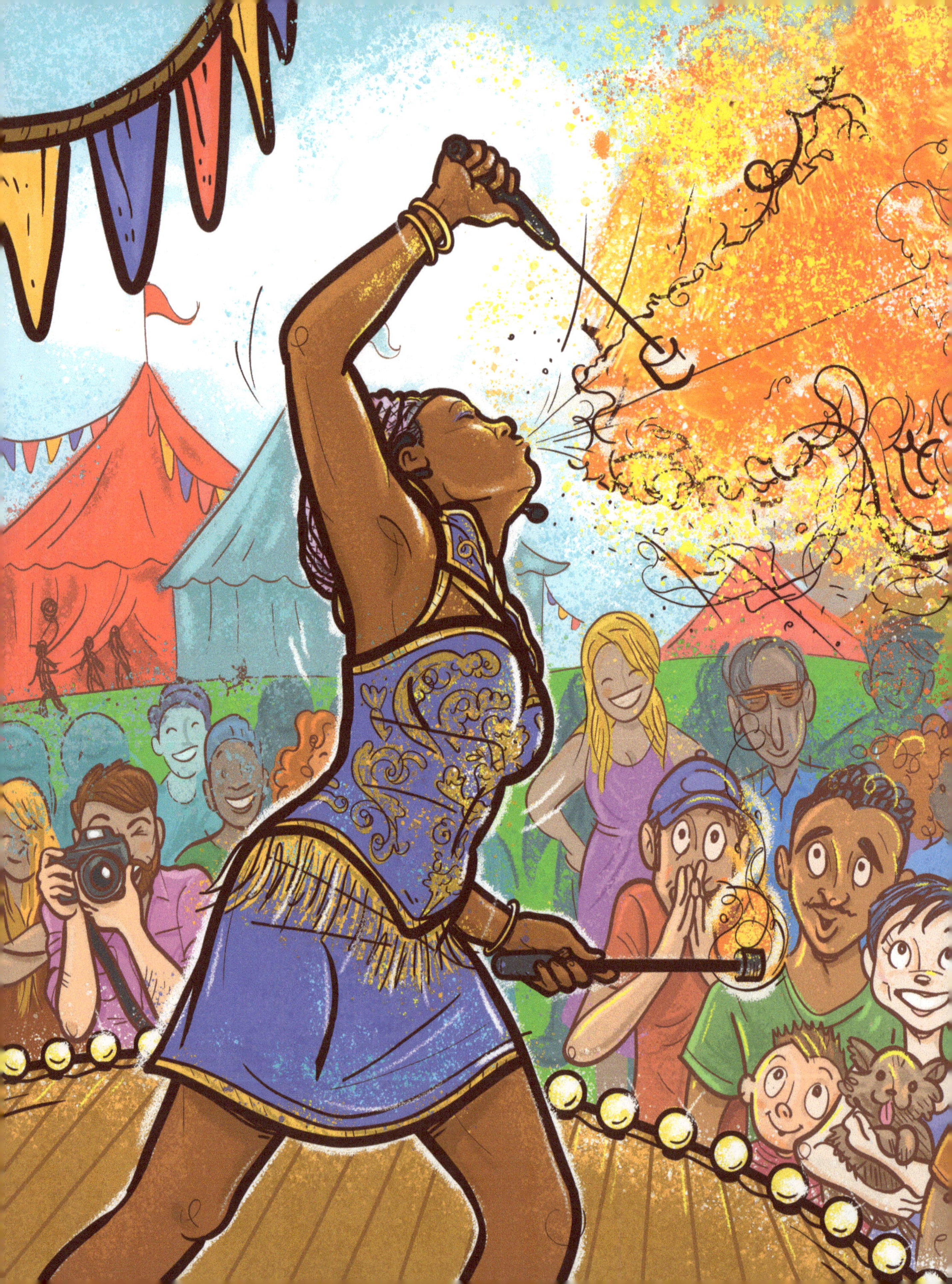

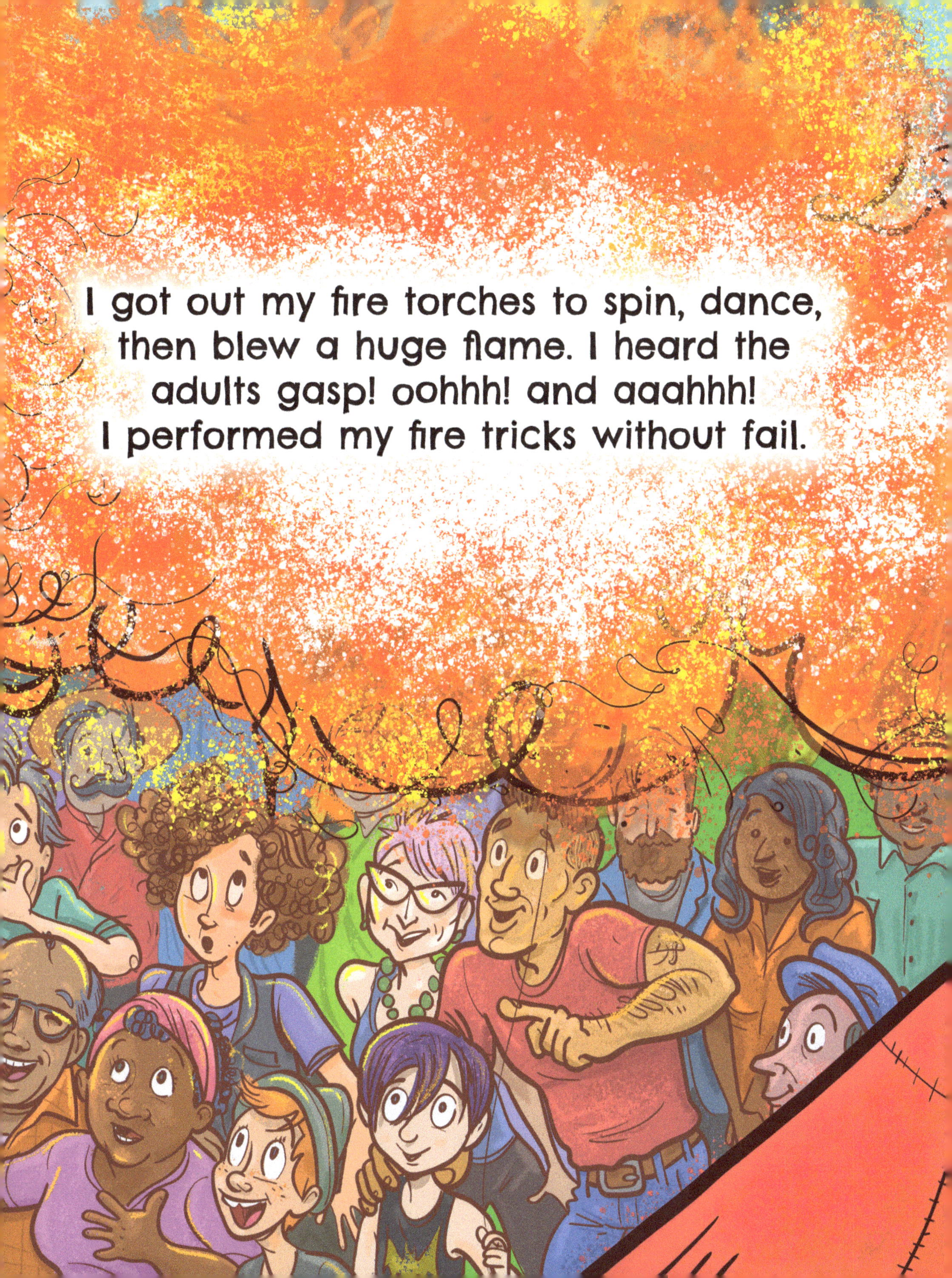

I got out my fire torches to spin, dance, then blew a huge flame. I heard the adults gasp! oohhh! and aaahhh! I performed my fire tricks without fail.

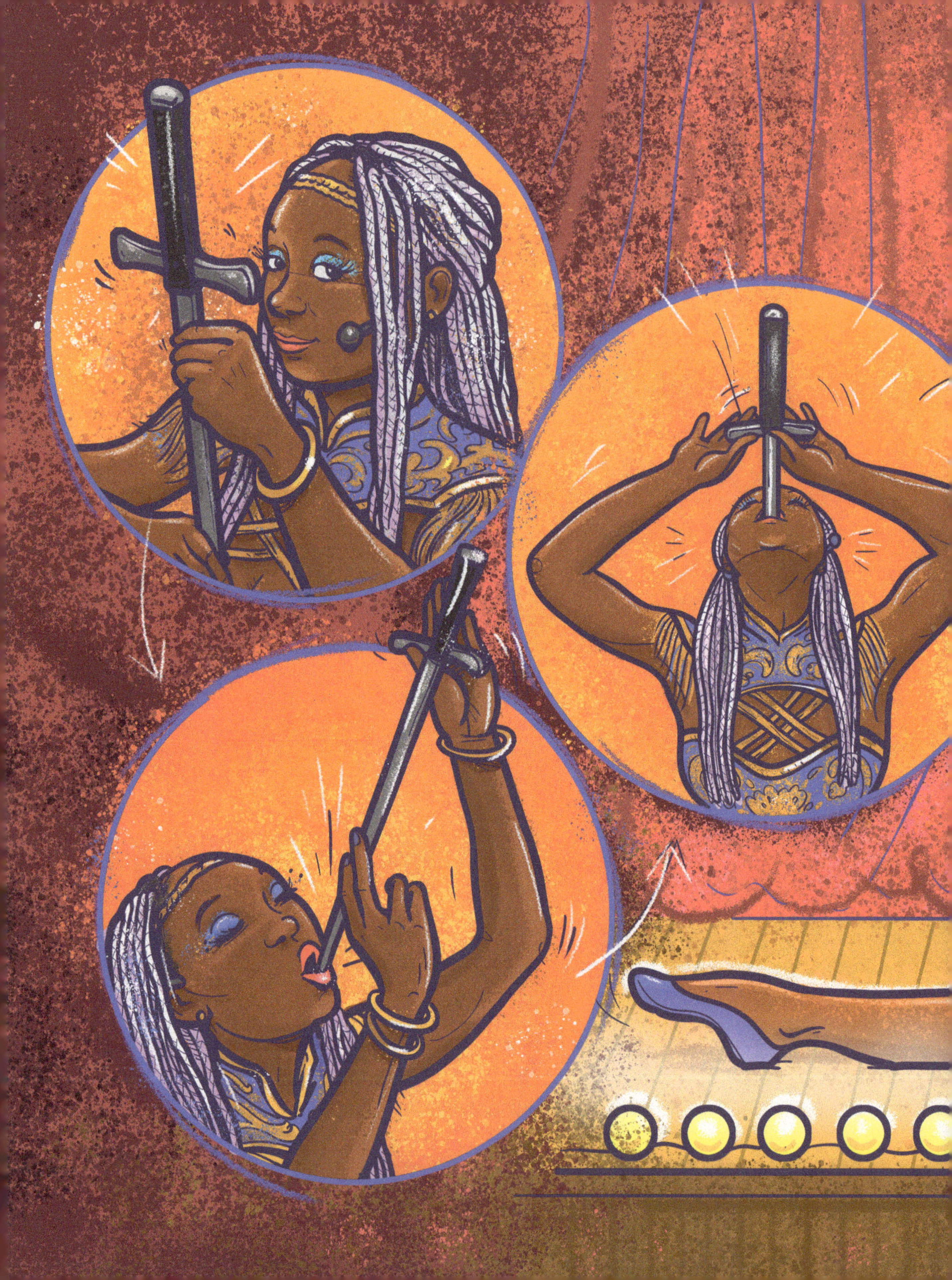

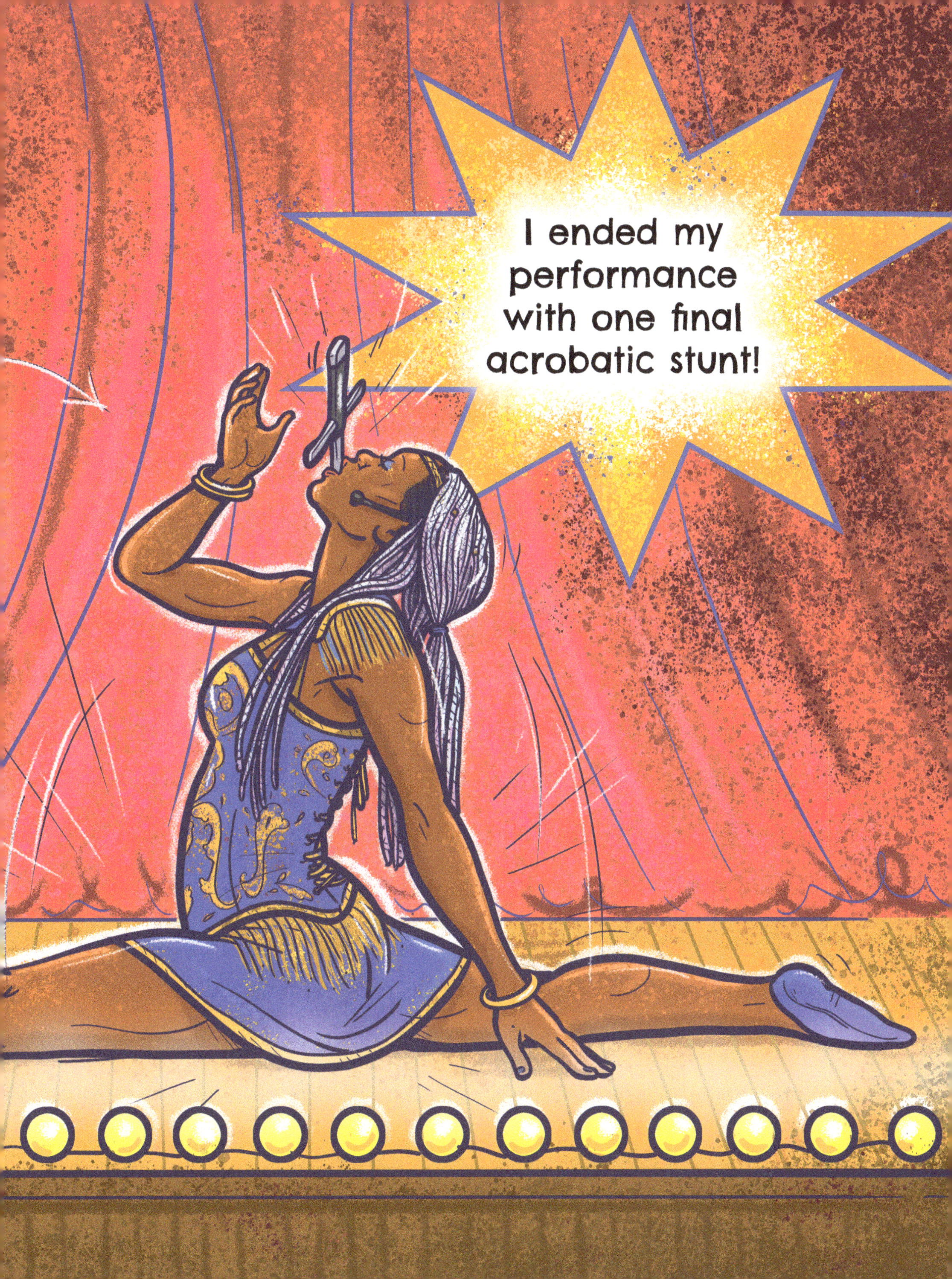
I ended my
performance
with one final
acrobatic stunt!

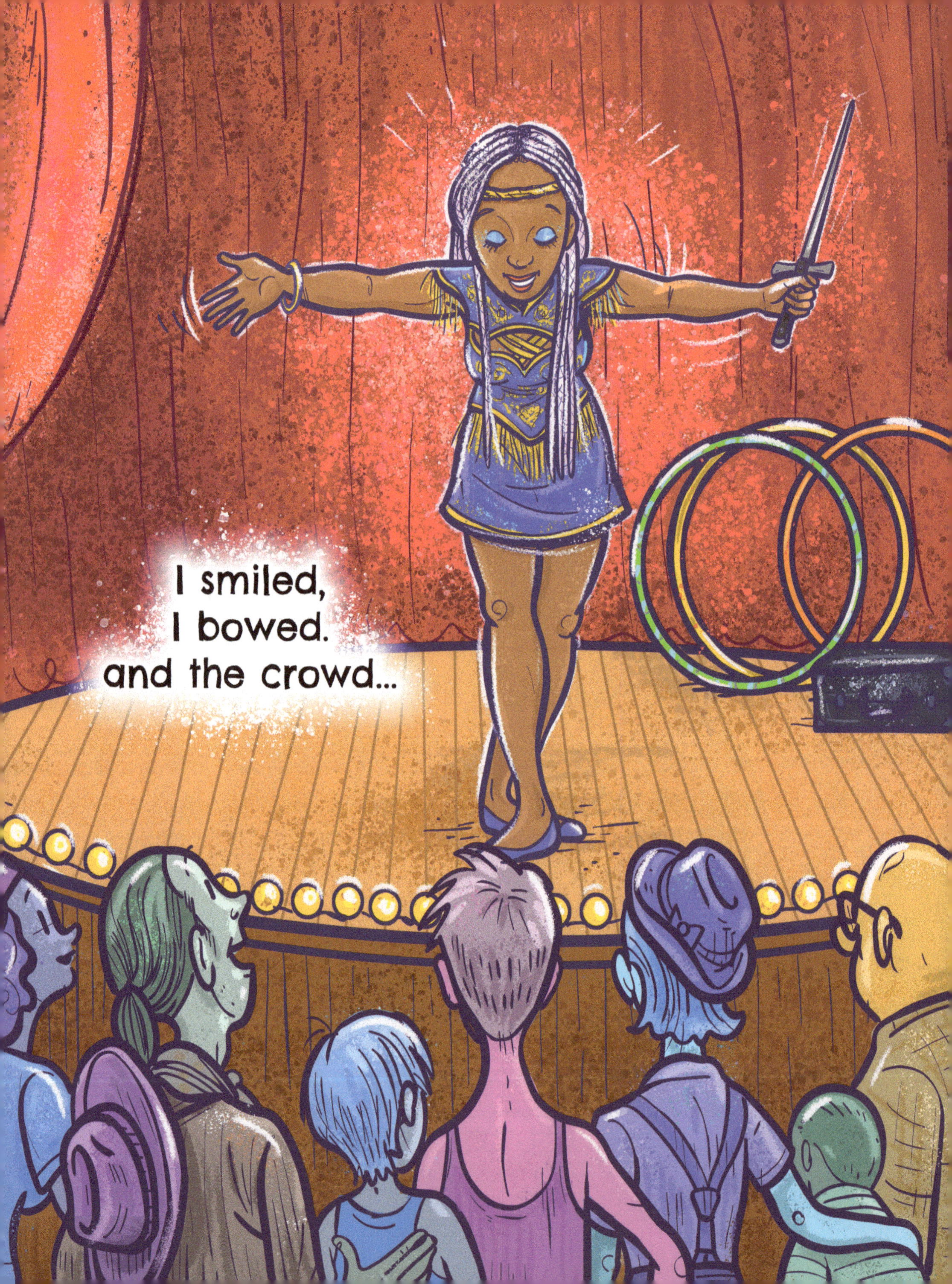

I smiled,
I bowed.
and the crowd...

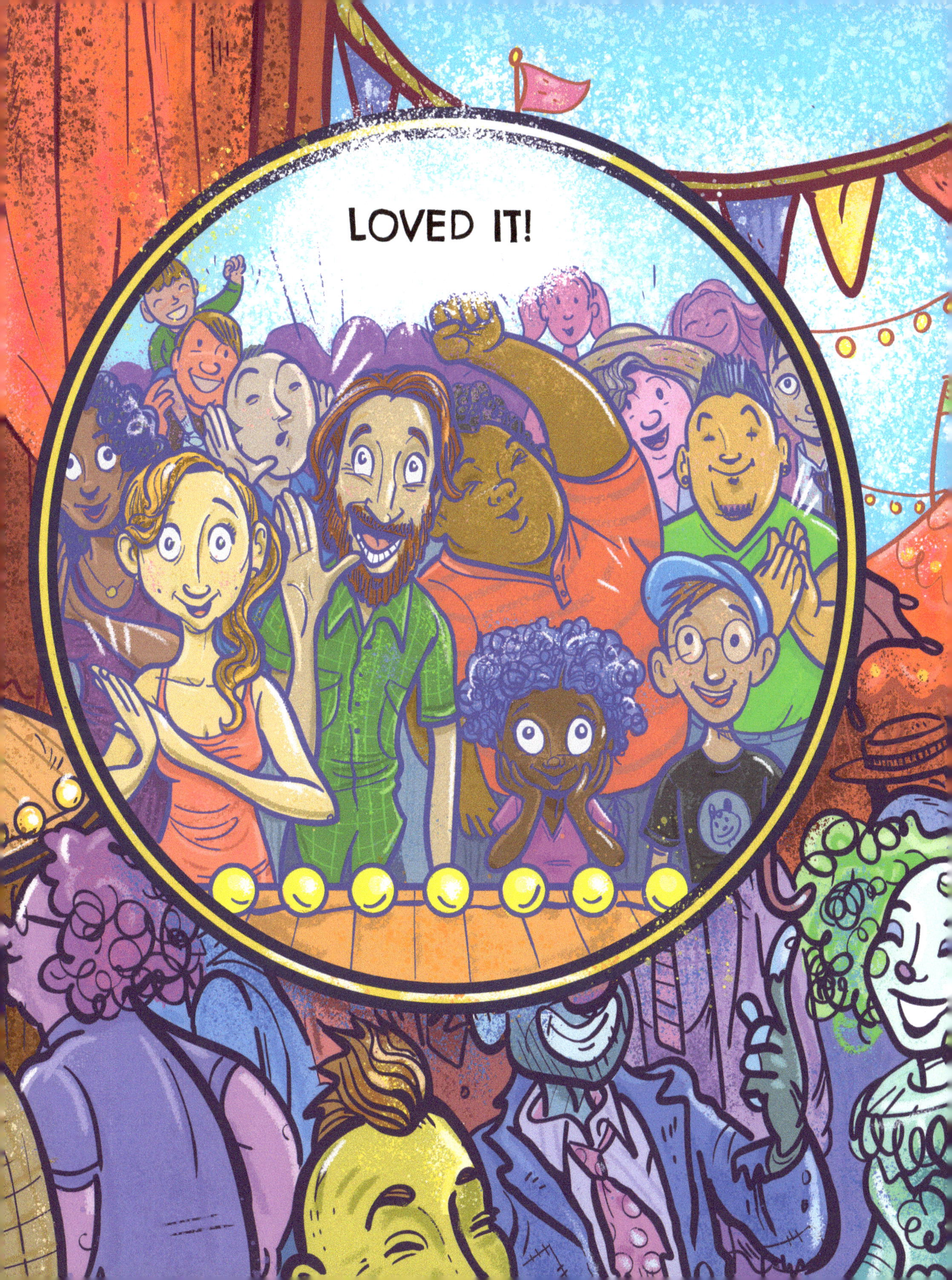

LOVED IT!

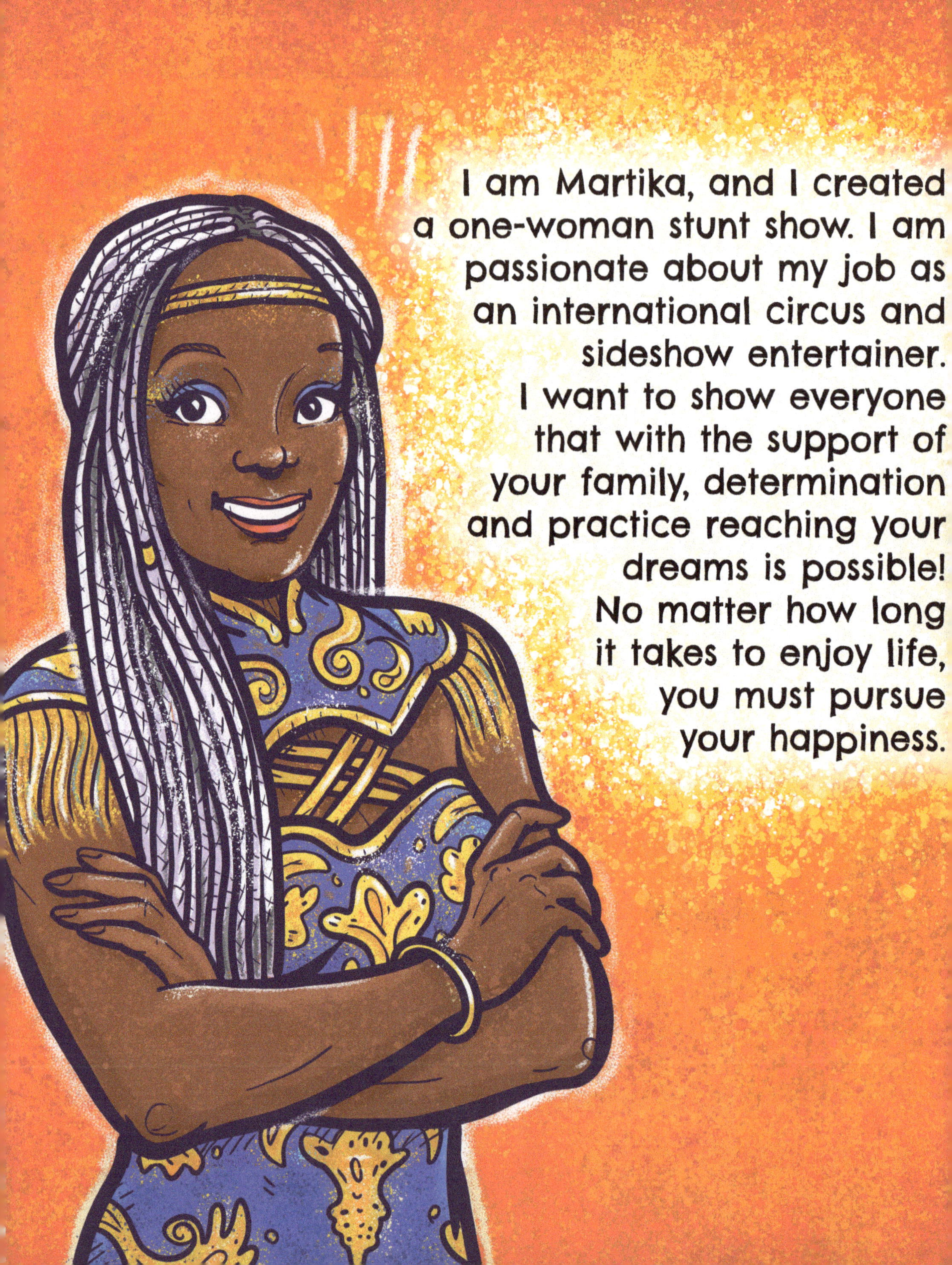

I am Martika, and I created a one-woman stunt show. I am passionate about my job as an international circus and sideshow entertainer.
I want to show everyone that with the support of your family, determination and practice reaching your dreams is possible!
No matter how long it takes to enjoy life, you must pursue your happiness.

About the Author

Martika Daniels is an entertainer and author based in Kansas City, Missouri. After discovering the circus arts at a young age, Martika has studied a variety of disciplines including dance, hula hoop, fire arts, and sideshow. She has performed her one-woman stunt show, delivered motivational speeches, and taught circus arts workshops around the world for over a decade.
The inspiration for *The Amazing Martika* came from a desire to share the spark that circus brought to her as a child.

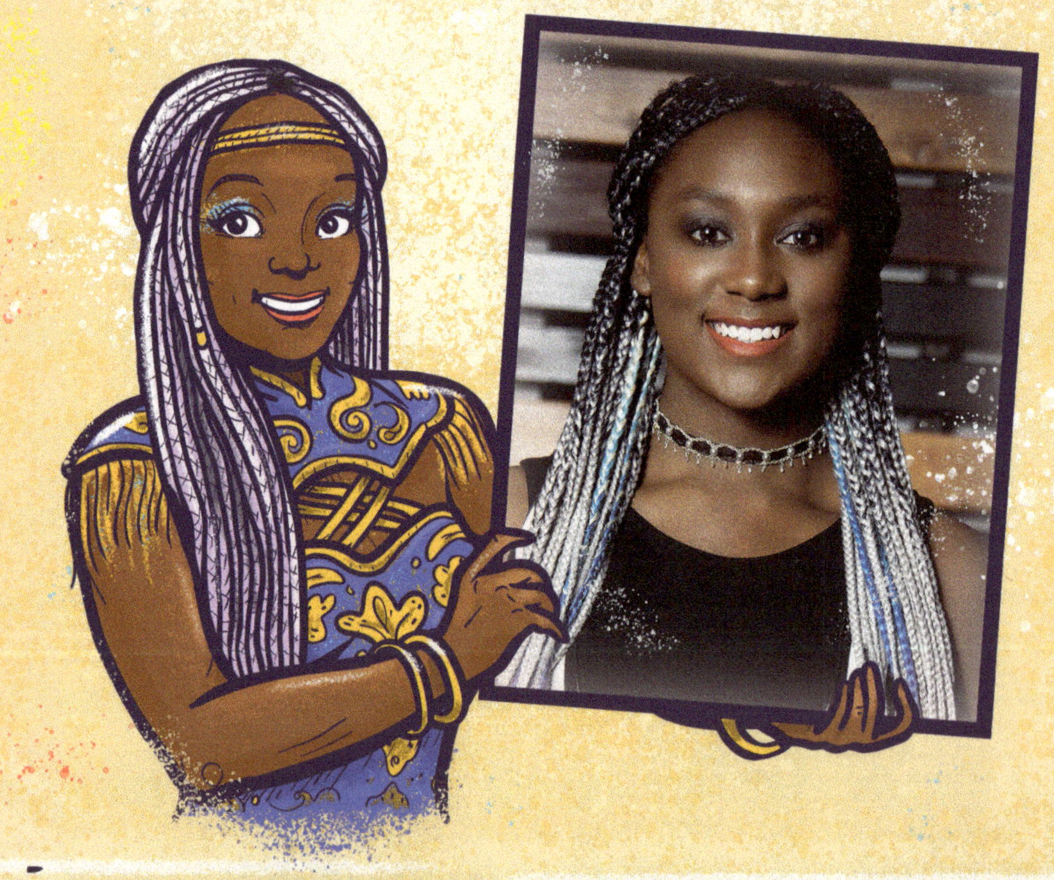

About the Illustrator

Damian Blake is an artist and entertainer based in Kansas City, Missouri. He has worked as a designer for corporations including Hallmark Cards, and illustrates for clients around the world. A performer since childhood, he has brought his love of clowning to stage roles, cabaret shows, and commercial work. He is also an accomplished Charlie Chaplin impersonator and historian, and has provided silent comedy from coast to coast.

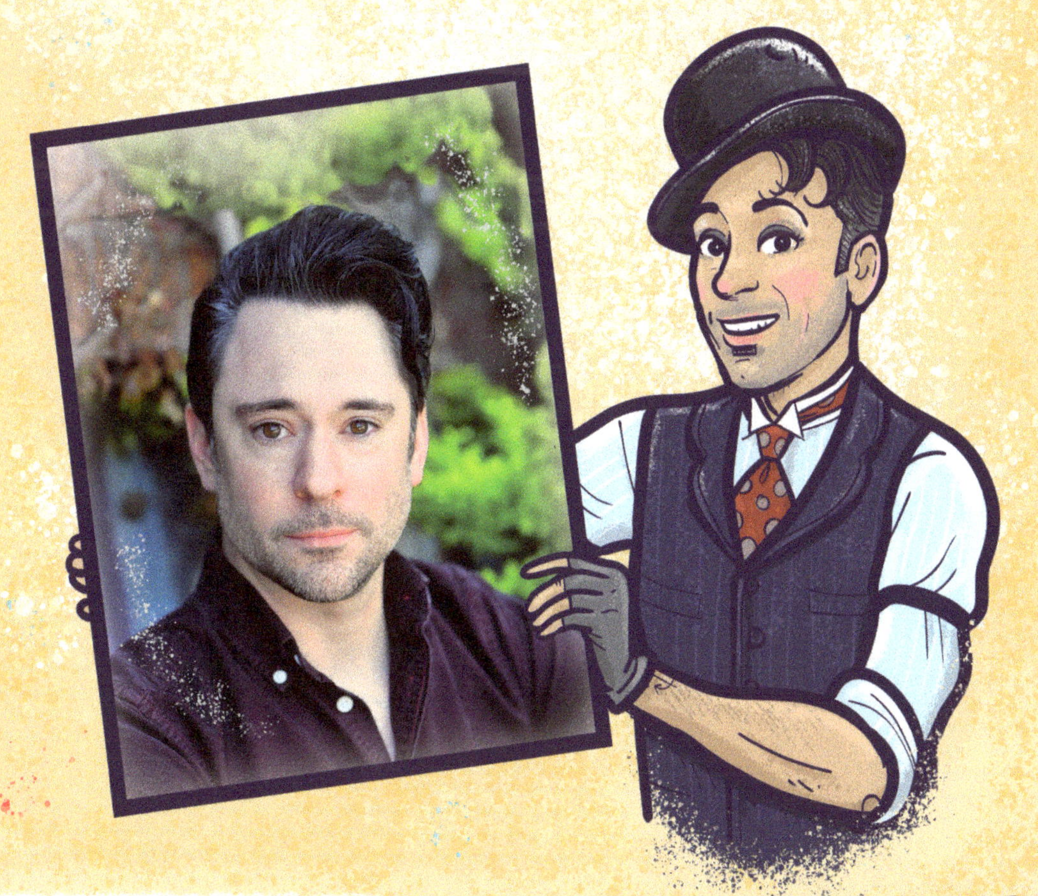

www.ingramcontent.com/pod-product-compliance
Lightning Source LLC
Chambersburg PA
CBHW041053050726
47599CB00018B/2141